Quilting by Design

155 Free-Motion Designs in 10 Elegant Suites

Jessica Schick

C&T PUBLISHING

Publisher: Amy Marson

Creative Director: Gailen Runge

Art Director: Kristy Zacharias

Editors: S. Michele Fry, Gailen Runge, and Lynn Koolish

Technical Editor: Susan Nelsen

Cover Designer: April Mostek

Book Designer: Kristen Yenche

Production Coordinator: Zinnia Heinzmann

Production Editor: Alice Mace Nakanishi

Illustrator: Jessica Schick

Photo Assistant: Mary Peyton Peppo

Photography by Diane Pedersen, unless otherwise noted

Published by C&T Publishing, Inc., P.O. Box 1456, Lafayette, CA 94549

Library of Congress Cataloging-in-Publication Data

Schick, Jessica, 1969-

Quilting by design : 155 free-motion designs in 10 elegant suites cover designer: April Mostek Book Designer: Kristen Yenche / illustrated by Jessica Schick.

pages cm

ISBN 978-1-60705-993-6 (softcover)

1. Patchwork--Patterns. 2. Patchwork quilts. 3. Quilting--Patterns. I. Title.

TT835.S334 2015

746.46--dc23

2014031105

Printed in China

10 9 8 7 6 5 4 3 2 1

Acknowledgments

Thank you to—

- My friend Karen Coss for providing the quilt top to show designs from the Olive Leaves suite.
- Sandy Carlile at Macy's for helping me with makeup for my photo.
- Karen McTavish for saying that if it's worth doing, it's probably not going to be easy. I've thought of those words many times over the years.
- My good friend Patricia Ritter, who kept telling me that I will be glad that I wrote this book once it's completed, and allowing me to whine about it while struggling with the parts of the process that are outside my wheelhouse.
- C&T Publishing for providing me with the opportunity to write this book.

Dedication

When we started dating, my husband, John, asked me what I wanted to do for a living if I could do anything I wanted. My reply was, "Anything, even if I don't think that I could ever make money doing it?" He said, "Yes, anything." I told him that I wanted to be able to draw for a living. He's spent more than two decades making sure this could happen, and several years ago that's exactly what happened. For this I'd like to thank him. Without his belief that I could actually do this and I could do it very well, I'd have never taken the steps to build a design business where I draw not only for myself but for other designers as well. I also want to thank him for years of ripping out stitches when things didn't go as planned. He calls himself my automatic seam ripper.

My family, friends, and customers have also been so supportive. I can't thank them enough.

Front cover: *Baroque Angels*, 38″ × 38″, by Jessica Schick

Uses wholecloth design from Suite 1: Baroque Florals and Angels (page 30). Jessica shaded areas of the quilt by hand with ebony pencil and then treated the quilt for permanency.

Contents

Introduction

Let me tell you a little about myself so that you know how the information in this book came about.

I've always drawn. I can't remember a time when I didn't draw or wasn't into art of some kind. But I always wanted to show people how many ways you can use just a few small elements to make wonderful elaborate designs. I also am the kind of person that has a hard time settling for an "inside the box" answer.

When I started quilting and wanted design patterns, I didn't want to settle for the size that they were drawn in. I wanted them to fit just right. To get the fit and style that I wanted, initially I used programs that I had for screen printing to resize and print the patterns that I'd drawn, or even ones that I'd purchased in print. Then I could print them in whatever size I really wanted.

When I found out about computerized quilting machines, I knew I wanted to digitize design patterns for those, too. As much as I love art, I probably like the math and mechanical design part of things just as much. The idea that a machine can take my drawing and do it over and over again is very appealing to me.

Because I'd been drawing designs for screen printing and embroidery, I figured I could draw them for quilting as well. I wanted to create design patterns that anyone could have the way they wanted in a size that they wanted. Again, did you notice how drawing patterns for screen printing and embroidery is along the same lines as computerized quilting? You draw once, manipulate, and have the machine make the same pattern thousands of times if you want. I have no idea why this is so appealing to me, but it is. It feels as though I was born to draw and then make those design patterns into formats that are usable over and over again and across many mediums. The image below shows an example of the sketching I do when I start to think about creating a pattern.

I love ornamental quilting styles. If I have the time, I like to do over-the-top quilting, and you'll see some of those designs in this book. But I tried to rein it in to give everyone something they'd find appealing to use.

I started quilting for hire, I think because up until the last couple of years I can honestly say my piecing was not good at all. So I naturally leaned toward quilting wholecloth or appliqué quilts I had made myself. I love pieced quilts, though, and could imagine how I would quilt them. So I quilted other people's pieced quilts. I understand quilting for yourself versus quilting for pay. I make sure that some of my patterns are suitable for the quilter who is quilting for hire as well as for the individual.

Last, the way I do things might not be the way you would do it, or the way your mom does it, or the way the quilt police told you to do it. The information is just what works or doesn't work for me. There are no quilt police in my world, and I'm barring your door from them at least while you read this book. So enjoy, and let all the ideas you have gather steam.

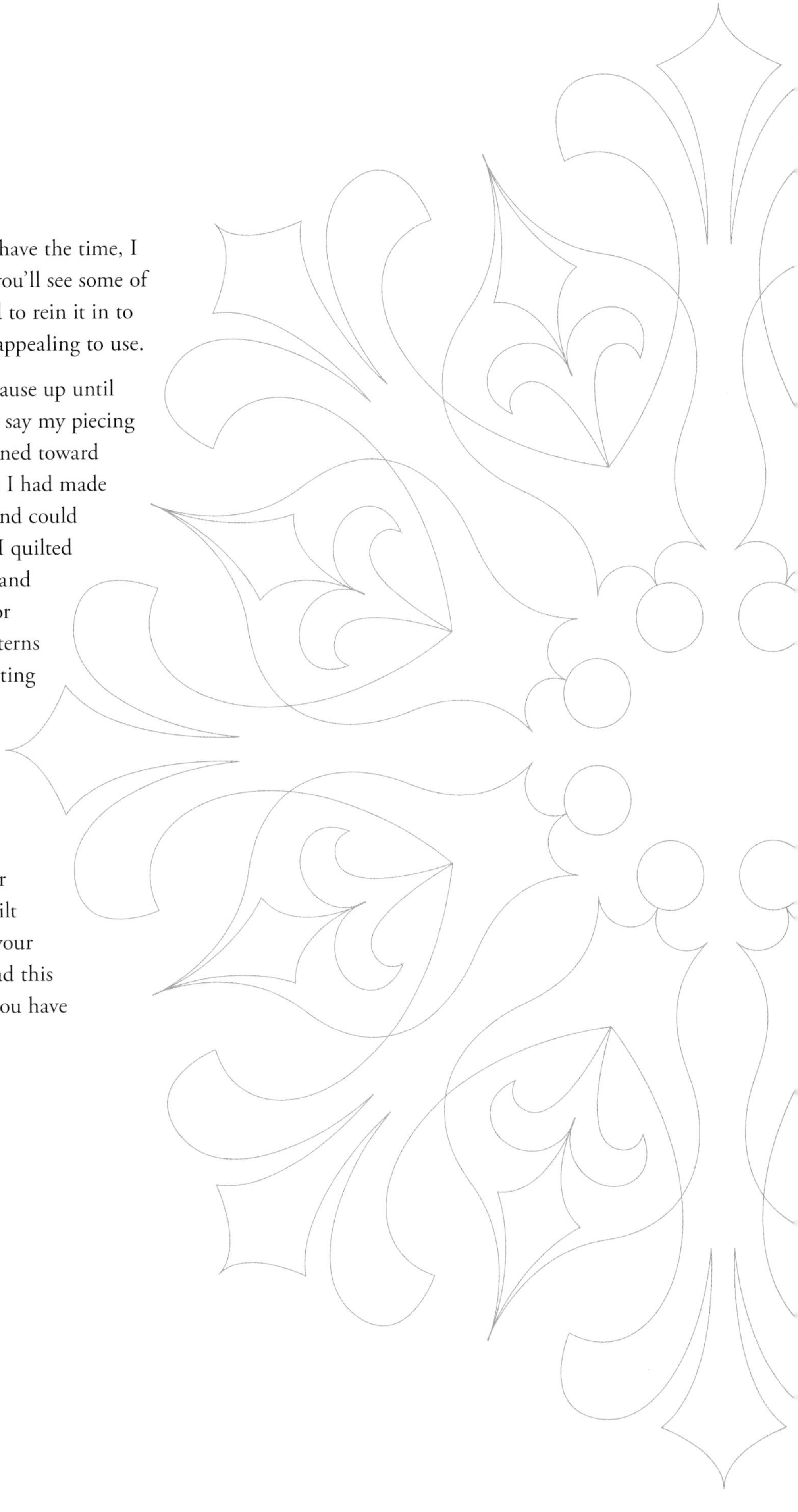

How to Use This Book

Regardless of whether you quilt by hand or use a domestic, midarm, or longarm machine, you can use the information in this book in a number of ways:

- You can copy (enlarging or reducing if desired) or trace the designs directly from the book pages.
- You can print the PDFs on the included CD, and then copy (enlarging or reducing, if desired) or trace the designs.
- You can copy the PDF files from the included CD onto your computer, and by resizing, combining, rotating, reflecting, and tweaking a few core design elements, create a wide variety of design patterns that will fit many different piecing shapes (see Customizing Design Patterns, page 10).
- If you have a computer-guided machine or embroidery machine, you can copy the machine-specific files from the included CD and use your software to create myriad design combinations to fit the size and space you are quilting.
- The quilting design patterns are presented in suites, but there is absolutely no reason why you can't combine elements from the different suites to suit your needs.

Plenty of books are available to show you how to get started quilting; with this book, I want to introduce you to ways that you can expand the use of design patterns—modifying them to fit, creating new combinations, and in general, exploring new options when it comes to quilting.

If you want to get more into creating your own designs, look at the Appendix: Making Design Patterns and Variations (page 120). You may be pleasantly surprised at how liberating it is to know that you can make whatever designs you need to fill your quilting design needs.

note **COPYRIGHT NOTE**

Quilting designs that you buy or download are often copyrighted! Even if you make changes to the design, if you are a commercial quilter and you plan to use designs on your customers' quilts from any patterns or modifications of patterns that you did not create, be sure to read the copyright information and make sure that the designer has granted permission to use the patterns for commercial use. Some may allow limited or unlimited commercial use, and some may not allow any commercial use.

If your client brings you this book as a source for quilting designs, you may reproduce as many designs as you wish on that client's quilt *only*. If your client does not own this book, the publisher and author encourage you to sell a copy to your client. Contact C&T Publishing (see back page) with your business name and resale number to purchase this book at a special resale price. For clients wishing to use designs from this book but not willing to purchase a copy, you may reproduce no more than 10 designs *total* for commercial purposes.

Planning Your Quilting

Have you noticed how hard it can be when looking for quilting patterns to find exactly what you are looking for? If you find a style that you like, the size and shape won't work. When you find the right shape and size, the style is all wrong. When you are looking for quilting design patterns, you don't always have to pick a pattern that fits the exact space you have. I say pick patterns in the style you like because you can often manipulate them to fit the space you have.

Breaking Up Is Easy to Do

One technique is to break up the space you are trying to fill so you can find patterns that are just what you want. A good example of this is a diamond, which is actually a parallelogram—not a lot of patterns out there fit this shape. When you come across spaces like this, consider breaking them up. These diamonds/parallelograms are actually two triangles. How many patterns can you find or make that are triangles? A lot!

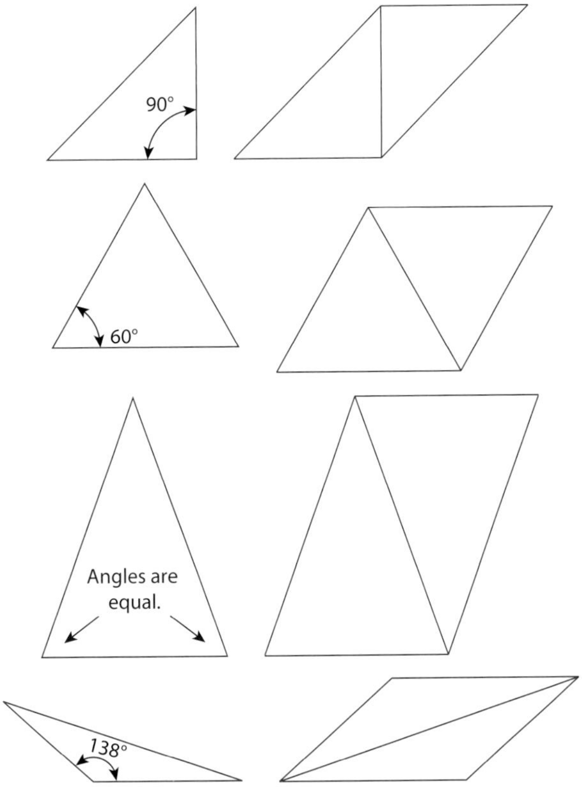

Splitting diamonds/parallelograms into triangles

Triangles are one of the most useful shapes you will come across when picking patterns to fill spaces or if you are designing your own patterns. If you can make a triangle out of something, you can probably manipulate it into any number of combinations until you find something that you like and that is usable.

Putting Together the Pieces

TRIANGLES

Many shapes are made up of triangles or triangles with other things attached to them. A Dresden Plate can be seen as triangles and may have triangles attached to the ends. Hexagons and octagons are also triangles put together. Most star blocks are made of triangles, or squares and triangles. And when you come right down to it, a square or rectangle can also be divided into at least two triangles. When you start to divide up an area, look for the triangles in that shape and you will have a much easier time finding patterns to go into it.

If you can't break a space apart, then maybe you need to combine two or more shapes to get a shape that is easier to find a design to fit.

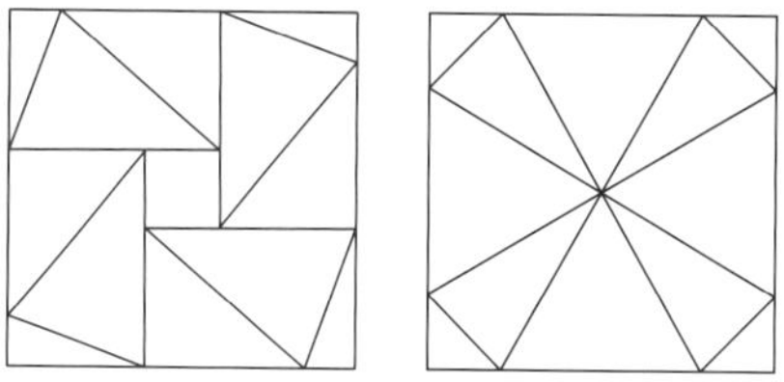

Also look for triangles when you start pulling apart designs, because if you can get a design down to a triangle as a core element, often you will find opportunities for new designs.

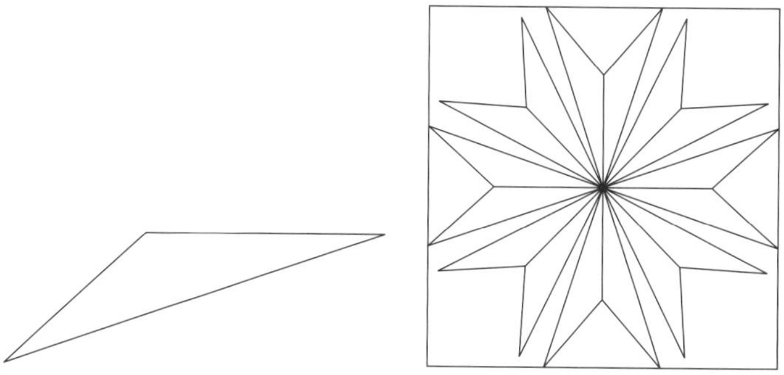

WEDGES, ARRAYS, AND CIRCULAR PATTERNS

I realize most of us don't piece too many circles, but if you start to look, you will see more shapes that are similar to circles or wedges. Take, for example, the Dresden Plate and Snowball blocks.

Wedges, arrays, and circular patterns can be great border patterns that give you a nice gentle curved edge, similar to a scalloped border. As you'll see in some of the patterns in this book, you can often turn a corner with a wedge or array pattern.

Simple Leaf Swag Continuous Triangle (JSBKPANTO801, page 97) is an example of a pattern that will give you a nice scalloped edge if you point the 90° angle of the triangle toward the center of the quilt.

Create scalloped quilt edges, or trim on red line for straight quilt edge.

Three wedge-shaped patterns will generally give you part of a circle or fan shape that will fit nicely turning a corner. Try it with Simple Leaf Element (JSBK8000, page 93). If you put the point of this element at 45° toward the center of the quilt, and then make two more copies, place them on each side of the original, and rotate them 22.5°, you will get a nice fan shape that can be used to turn a corner as an alternative to using a pattern that is specifically designed to fit a corner area.

Creating a fan shape for a corner

By using these patterns, you can quilt a border and then cut a small distance away from it to make any kind of edging shape that you like. As an added bonus, if you use wedges or arrays in the corners of a quilt, you won't necessarily need a 90° corner to bind; you can trim the quilt following the curve and have an easy edge to bind.

> **tip** Use the ideas in these examples anytime you have a challenging space to fill with quilting designs. The process works for many shapes—just look at the shapes of the designs you want to use and see how you can break up the space you have to make it work.

Conquering Wholecloth

Have you ever tried to quilt a wholecloth quilt, starting from the top, trying to make everything land where it is supposed to land—which it rarely does? Or have you just avoided the whole thing because it's too daunting? It doesn't have to be that way.

DIVIDE AND CONQUER

Instead of struggling, create spaces that you can fill with designs; in other words, design it as if you were quilting a pieced quilt. Divide up the space—into blocks, or a center medallion with some borders and corners, or cornerstones, or some triangles—and go from there. After you read Customizing Design Patterns (page 10), you'll be ready for Designing a Wholecloth Quilt (page 18).

Customizing Design Patterns

To make patterns from this book (and any other sources) fit your quilt perfectly, you probably need to resize and customize them. You can use a home printer or copier with an enlargement and reduction function, or you can take them to a copy shop to resize in a printout. But with your computer, you can open a whole new world of quilting designs! Using a computer graphics program on your computer, you can change the size, shape, and more so that the patterns fit *your* quilt without purchasing the same pattern at a different size or manually resizing and retracing.

PREVIEWING QUILT PATTERNS ON YOUR QUILT TOP

So how do you know what fits and what doesn't, what you need to customize, and what will work as is? There are many ways to visualize how quilting designs will fit onto a quilt. Some people draw on clear vinyl and place it over the quilt. You could also print quilting designs on paper and place them on your quilt top—but then you can't see the quilt underneath. To get the big picture, I find it easier to do this electronically.

Graphic design programs usually allow you to work in layers. Think of it as using pieces of tracing paper that you place on top of each other; each has a different portion of a design on it, but when you stack them, you can see the whole design through all the layers.

Take a photo of the quilt top and use that as the first layer; then add quilting designs on top in layers, moving them and resizing them as needed until you know how you will quilt the quilt. When deciding on patterns to use, think about how the spaces can be broken up (see Breaking Up Is Easy to Do, page 7).

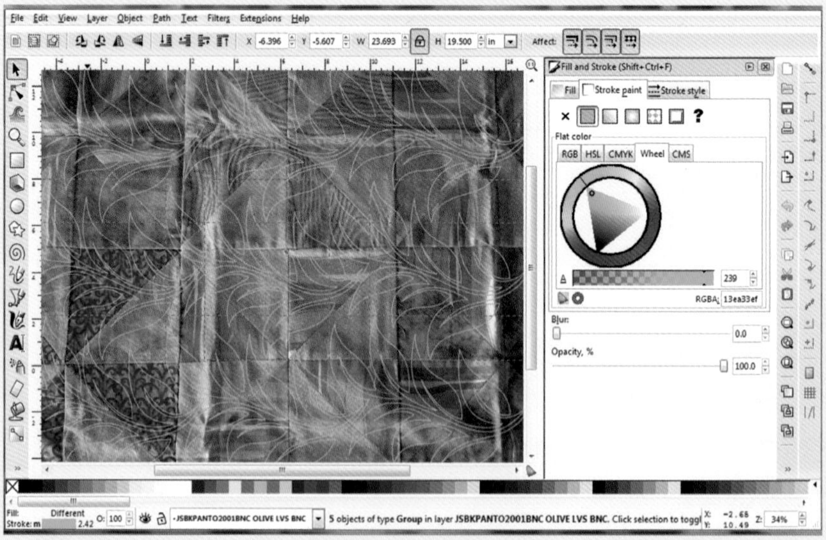

Plan quilting designs by layering them over photo of quilt top in computer graphic design program.

All the design files on the CD with this book have a transparent background, so you can layer them on top of a quilt photo and plan all your quilting.

Refer to the specific instructions on using layers in your graphic design program.

Computer Graphic Design Programs

Graphic design programs are great, and there's no reason why you can't learn the basics so you can make quilting more fun for yourself. No more settling for a design that is *almost* the right size or shape, or spending hours manually tracing patterns over and over so you have enough of them to complete your project.

Two programs you can download for free are Inkscape and Apache OpenOffice, which is a productivity suite that includes a drawing program called Draw. Both are suitable for resizing and printing patterns. OpenOffice Draw is a little easier navigate than Inkscape. However, it usually takes longer for the OpenOffice suite to download. Also, OpenOffice can be confusing for people who are less familiar with technology, because to allow the Draw program to open and manipulate the PDF files that are on the CD included with this book, you have to download and install a separate plug-in.

Inkscape is a good program with strong drawing tools. It's similar in many ways to CorelDRAW or Adobe Illustrator. It downloads quickly, but some users say the program makes their computer perform more slowly after they run it. However, this would be the case with most graphic design programs. Basically, if you have an older computer and/or limited RAM and processor speed, you might experience some slowing down if you try to run other programs at the same time as a graphics program or a computer-aided design (CAD) program. Whatever graphic design program you decide to use, refer to the program's manual for specifics. The next few pages will give you some ideas for graphic design applications to use with your quilting designs.

The key to working with these programs with designs is using true vector artwork files rather than raster images (see Meet Raster and Vector, below). Vector artwork will allow you to manipulate the actual lines of the artwork—not just make a picture of it larger or smaller.

By using vector artwork you can resize items without any loss in quality. You can adjust the stroke (line) weight, which means you can make a design larger and not have the line get thicker unless you want it to be thicker. You can copy and paste multiple elements, and cut apart designs to create new elements. You can do a lot of other things too, but for the purposes of quilting designs you need to learn only a few basic transformation tools—how to rotate, resize, cut, paste, divide, and group/ungroup. It doesn't matter what program you use as long as it will read and allow editing of vector artwork.

MEET RASTER AND VECTOR

Computer graphics programs create artwork using either raster graphics or vector graphics.

Often when you see a photo or other image in a computer program, you are looking at an image composed of a pattern of pixels (the pattern is also referred to as a *bitmap*). When you enlarge the image, eventually you can see those pixels, and the image appears blurry. Raster graphics, common in paint and photography programs, use pixels.

Drawing programs, on the other hand, often use vector graphics, which are best for creating and manipulating quilting designs. Raster graphics use pixels to make shapes; vector graphics use paths (also called *strokes*) to create the image. Instead of constructing your drawn lines from pixels, vector graphics use the lines themselves.

Vector graphics make it easier to resize and stretch images. Because the images are not made of pixels, they can be printed at any size while also maintaining their smooth lines.

To view and print vector graphics files on different devices, you can create a PDF (portable document format) file. The PDF is an image of the drawing that appears on any monitor or printer as it was created. To view a PDF, you do not need the program that originally created the image.

tip If you have some version of Photoshop or Photoshop Elements on your computer (maybe because it came with your camera), it may or may not allow you to edit in the way I'm describing. Photoshop will allow you to open many formats that contain vector artwork, but for many of them it limits the amount of vector editing available. Other programs may open some of the formats provided on the CD at the back of the book, but they may read them as raster images, which won't allow you to edit the patterns as I'm describing.

FILE FORMATS

The graphics files on the accompanying CD are vector artwork with editing capabilities available, provided you are using the correct programs to open them. Files are provided as PDFs. (SVG formats also are often available from other sources and can be opened in many graphic design programs.)

The following is a short list of some of the graphic design software that you can use with these file formats: Inkscape, OpenOffice Draw, CorelDRAW, Adobe Illustrator, and several CAD programs.

Note that the PDF files on the CD at the back of the book were created so that you can edit them, but other types of PDF files are available—they can be written so they contain either raster images or vector artwork. If they contain vector artwork, they need to be written with the editing capabilities available, not locked. The best way to find out if a file you have available is vector artwork or if the editing capabilities are locked is to try out a file from the pattern source you are using. Many websites allow a free download of a pattern.

tip Always save all the file formats you receive for designs you purchase. If you later add a computerized quilting system to your quilting machine, then you may need those design files in a format not listed in this discussion. Since none of us knows what the future holds, it's wise to save all the formats.

Resizing a Pattern

Let's use Inkscape and one of the PDFs from the included CD for our examples. The process is similar in many other programs, and you can download Inkscape for free, so you can follow along if you like.

NOTE: The specific instructions and images showing how to use the software are based on the version of the program that was available at the time of writing. However, software is often updated, so later versions may not work or look exactly the same, but the general process will be the same for newer versions as well as for other graphic design programs.

GETTING STARTED

1. If you don't already have a graphic design program on your computer, install the program of your choice.

NOTE: Inkscape (and other programs) that were originally designed to run on a PC require a few additional setup steps to run on a Mac.

2. Open the program before you open any file. We'll be using a PDF, and you may have more than one program that will open PDF files, so you want to open the file in the program you want to use.

3. Select a pattern from the CD and transfer it to your computer. You can do this using Copy and Paste commands or drag and drop. If you are unsure how to copy and paste a file, follow the instructions in the Help menu or one of the many online resources.

OPENING THE PATTERN FILE

1. In Inkscape (or your chosen graphic design program), from the menu bar select File > Open, find the PDF file you want, and click the file name to open it.

2. A pop-up window will open. Leave the settings as shown unless you are importing text you want to create as outlines; if that's the case, then change the setting for Text Handling.

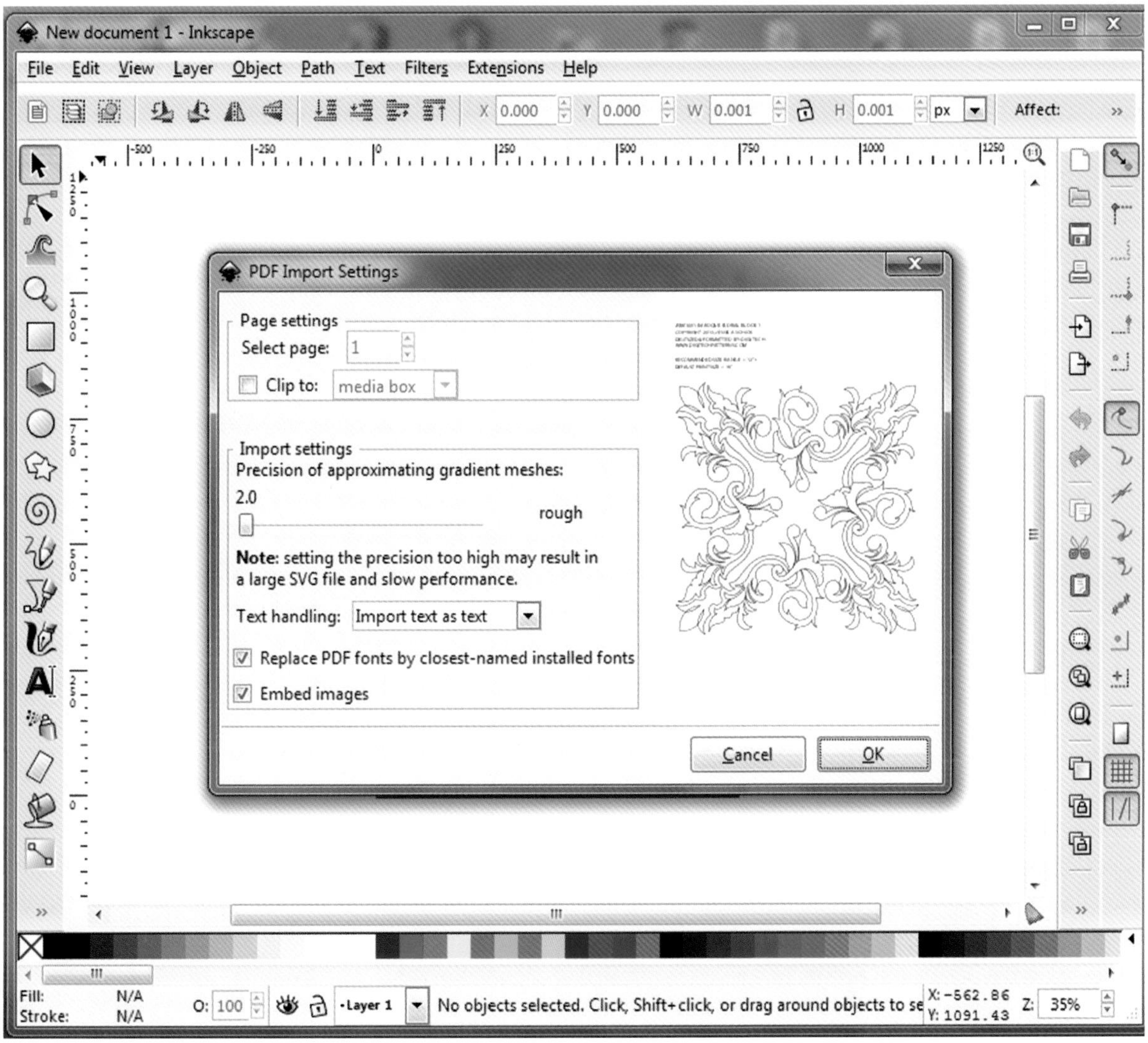

Pop-up window appears when PDF file is opened.

3. IMPORTANT: *Save the file with a new name so you can keep track of both the original file and your new, modified file.*

4. To make your life easier when it comes time to print the pattern, from the menu bar select File > Document Properties > Page to set the page size to the largest size paper that you have and that your printer will accommodate. But don't worry if your design is larger than the page; you'll learn how to print it in Printing Your Pattern (page 21). While you are in that screen, make sure Default Units is set to "in" (for inches).

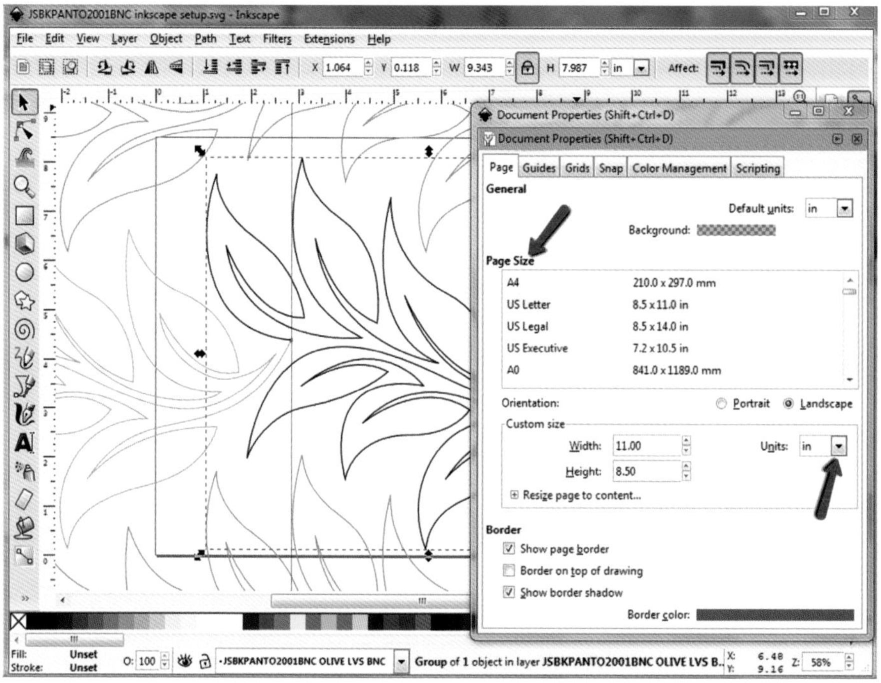

Setting page size to match paper size and default units to inches

SELECTING THE OBJECT

When working with vector graphics, you need to select the specific lines you want to work with. When artwork comes into the program, it will usually come in grouped together; therefore, you will need to ungroup the objects so that you can resize the pattern or just the elements you want to work with.

1. Select an object by clicking on the lines of the artwork or text; or, using the Selection tool (the black arrow), click and drag the cursor to include all the items that you want to select. You'll know it's selected when you see dashed lines around the object with arrows on the outside.

Selected item surrounded by dashed lines

2. To ungroup, click on the selected object and from the menu bar select Object > Ungroup. You can also right-click on the selected object and then click Ungroup. You may have to ungroup several times to get down to just the element you want to edit or resize.

tip If you have multiple elements from the original design and you are using only one of them, select and delete the elements you don't need. However, do keep the header and copyright information—not only to keep the copyright with the pattern for designers, but also to help you know what pattern you have printed, where you got it, where to find help if you need it, and where to get more if you like it.

RESIZING THE DESIGN ELEMENT

1. Select the item you want to resize by clicking on it.

2. Then you can either pull on the arrows on the outside of the selection box or you can use the Properties boxes and type in the size that you want. It's as simple as that.

You can control the proportional height and width using the lock near the Size Properties boxes. You can toggle between locked and unlocked by clicking on the icon. (Locks or check boxes to maintain proportion are generally near the boxes that indicate the size of the selected objects.)

- If you want the height and width to change relative to each other, close the lock. For example, if you change the height of an object, the length will automatically change proportionally.
- If you want to change the height without changing the width, or change the width without changing the height, open the lock.

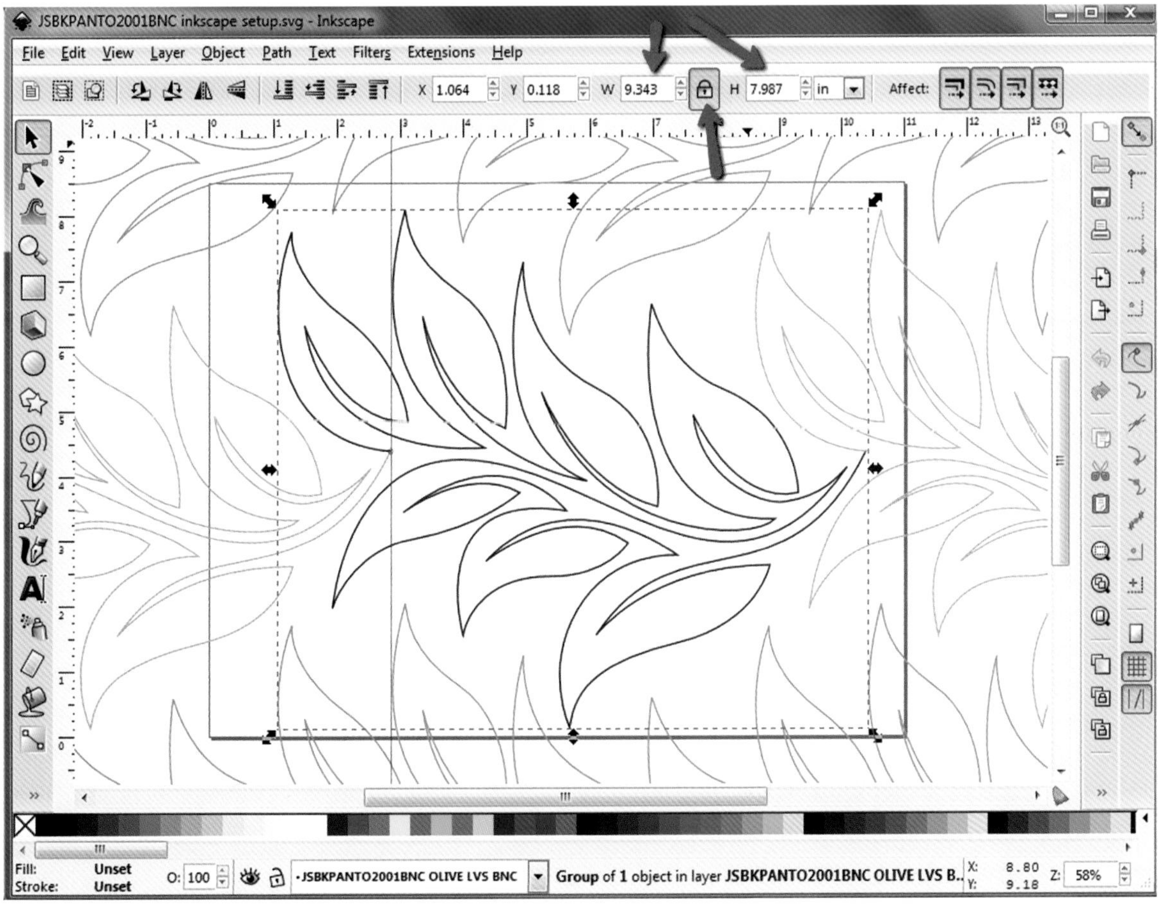

Properties boxes for resizing objects

Creating Pantographs

The two basic types of quilting patterns are *motifs* and *repeats*. Motifs are stand-alone designs (imagine something you would quilt contained within a quilt block). Repeats are designs that can flow into a long pattern that can be quilted in a continuous line, or they can be design elements repeated over and over to create a unified look (think of something you would quilt inside a border). If they form a continuous line of stitching, I refer to them as *pantographs*.

Rows of pantographs can often nest together so the rows gracefully stack to create an allover pattern. In pantographs, the row you are quilting runs down the center of the strip, and partial rows above and below are used for placement when you nest rows together. You can create your own pantographs easily using a design program. Such a program allows you to duplicate the design into a continuous flow of the repeat, stack copies to see how they nest, and change the color of the lines to make it easy to follow.

Here's how to set up the repeat:

1. Select the object you want to copy, and then from the menu bar, select Edit > Copy, then Edit > Paste. The copy will appear. Select Edit > Paste one more time, so that you will have three copies of the pattern repeat to work with. Change the stroke color of the repeats on either side of the original so you will be able to tell them apart from the main row. To change the stroke color, select the repeat, and then on the menu bar select Object > Fill and Stroke, and a pop-up menu will appear. If you use a shade of gray you can still print the pattern in black and white.

> **tip** If you don't see the Fill and Stroke options on the screen, from the menu bar select Object > Fill and Stroke. There are three tabs: Fill, Stroke Color, and Stroke Style.

2. Align the three repeats by holding the shift key and clicking on each repeat. Then on the menu bar, select Object and near the bottom of the drop-down list click Align and Distribute. In the pop-up menu, you can center and align the image perfectly by aligning it horizontally and distribute it vertically. Then group the three repeats together to create the row for nesting.

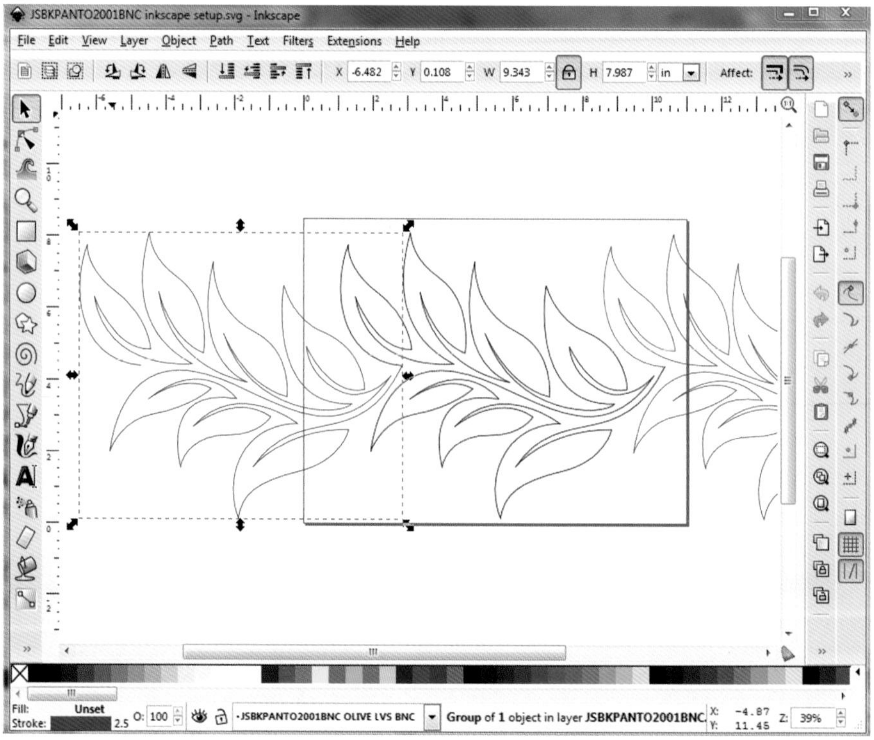

Creating repeats, changing stroke color, and grouping

3. Make two copies of the row to paste above and below the original row. Align and distribute the three rows. Group these rows together.

4. Copy the row repeats you just created, paste them to the left and right of the original repeat, and make them a different color. This will give you a reference to align your pages side by side if you are printing a pantograph that is larger than the width of one standard page. The number of repeats you can string together depends on the paper and pattern size. If you have room, I recommend making at least a partial copy of the repeat for placement. Repeat the steps for creating the repeated rows, grouping all the repeats together.

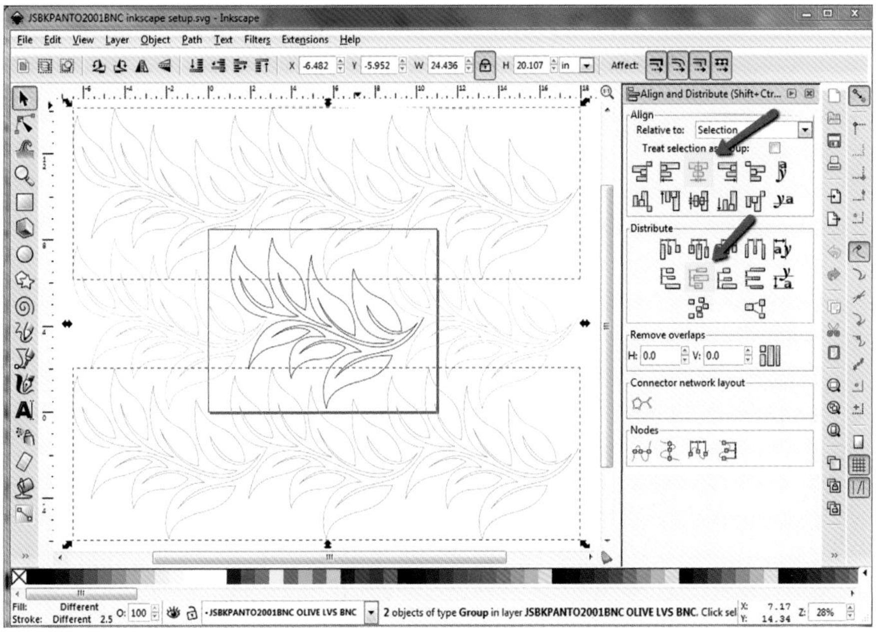

Copying, aligning, and grouping rows

tip

When working with Inkscape—

- To select a number of objects, hold the Shift key while clicking on the individual objects.
- To move an object in small increments, select the object and then use the keyboard arrow keys.

Designing a Wholecloth Quilt

With the skills you've learned in this chapter for customizing designs, you're ready to design a wholecloth quilt.

NOTE: The following sequence uses the Baroque Floral and Angels set (page 30).

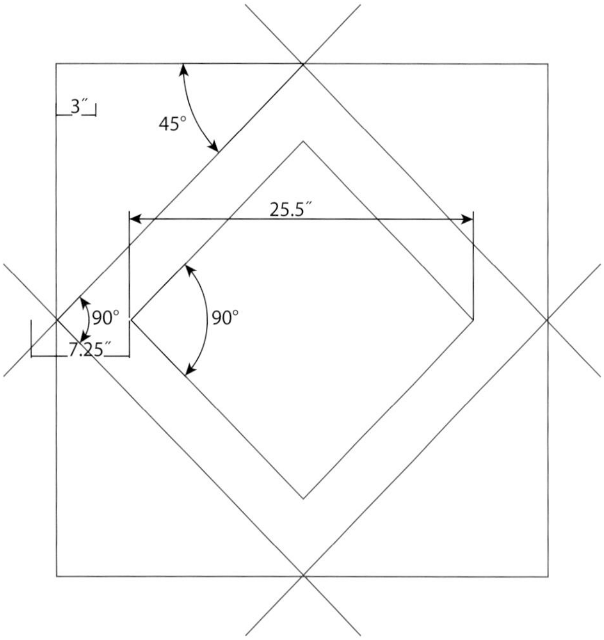

Look at your quilt, and sketch out some ideas of how you can break up the space into areas you can fill—squares, rectangles, and triangles. When you have your final design, mark and then baste (see Basting, page 26) these areas.

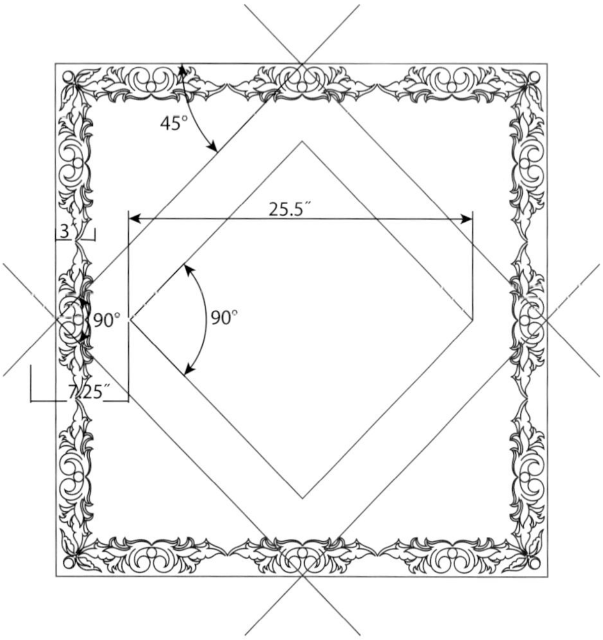

Starting with the outer border, choose a pattern you can use multiples of to fill the border space. Remember you can make adjustments as needed (see Customizing Design Patterns, page 10). Copy and paste as needed to fill the space. Don't forget the corners.

Add the center element(s). In this example a triangular design is repeated four times to fill the center diamond.

The design element from the center is also used in the corners.

The border design element is sized and repeated to surround the center diamond.

The final element is a pair of simple straight lines to fill in just inside the outer border.

More Editing Options

If you have resized the pattern—motif or repeating—significantly, you may want to change the stroke weight. If you've enlarged the design, the original line weight might be too light to easily follow. If you've reduced the design, the stroke might be too heavy and thick. You can make partial rows used for placement dashed or dotted instead of a different color, if you prefer that. These changes can be made by clicking on the Stroke Style tab to bring up the pop-up menu.

The most readable stroke size for patterns is 1–2 points; make sure the unit for strokes is set to "pt" (for points). Select the lines you want to change, click the Down arrow next to the window to the right of the stroke width, and select the stroke size you want. If you are going to put the pattern under the fabric and trace it, a 2-point line weight is good. If you are going to put the pattern on top of the fabric and stitch through it, a 1-point line is best.

If you want a dashed or dotted line, select the item you want to change, and then select from the line type options presented in the Stroke Style tab. You can also select the length of the dash and the gap between the dashes in the window to the right of the stroke selection menu.

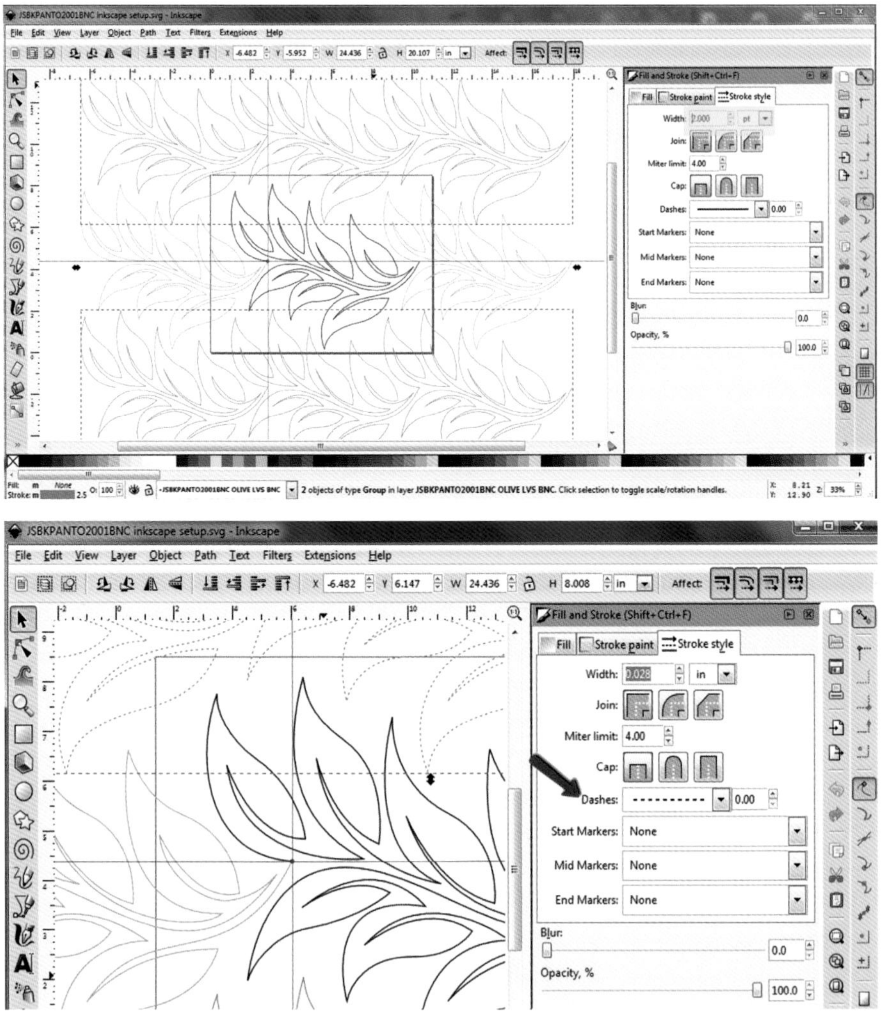

Changing stroke style

tip Now that you know how to use graphic design software, in addition to changing designs that have already been created, you can also create your own designs (see Appendix: Making Design Patterns and Variations, page 120).

Finishing Up

GROUP THE ELEMENTS

After you have a pattern arranged the way you'd like, select all the elements and group them. This will prevent them from separating or realigning accidentally if you try to move things around for printing. Then save your pattern with a new file name.

CHECK THE PATTERNS FOR SCALE

Before you print your patterns and use them to quilt, it's important to check the pattern layout for appropriate scale. Make sure the design patterns work in relation to each other and that the overall quilting design works with the quilt.

Using a computer to size and manipulate your designs is very convenient, but you can also lose sight of the actual size of the designs. If you have used a graphic design program to preview your designs (see Previewing Quilt Patterns on Your Quilt Top, page 10), you should have a good idea of how your selected patterns are working. You may even want to make the quilt layer invisible so you see only the quilting designs. Take your time to look at the overall quilt and make sure that everything is working well together.

When you get ready to print, make sure you print the design patterns at the correct size to fit the desired areas of the quilt. Again, when using a computer, it's easy to forget to check the actual size of the design printouts.

Printing Your Pattern

There are many options for printing, but they vary depending on your printer. Every printer comes with its own software, so you'll need to explore the software to get the most out of your printer. Do some experimenting—you may find that your printer has more options available that will make this part of the process more efficient.

PRINTING ON PAPER

Printing on standard copier/printer paper is fine if you are going to follow the design pattern with a laser or stylus. Printing on legal-size paper will allow you to print larger sections of pattern with less work. You can stitch through the paper, but often a lot of little paper bits will remain stuck under the stitches.

tip Printing on paper designed for foundation paper piecing (such as Carol Doak's Foundation Paper by C&T Publishing) can alleviate some of the problems that occur when using regular printer paper because the paper is designed to be torn away.

PRINTING ON STABILIZER

An alternative to printing on regular copier paper is printing on tear-away stabilizers used for embroidery. This will allow you to stitch through the design while it's placed on the quilt top and then tear it away when finished. You can also print on some stabilizers that are both tear-away and wash-away. This is great because you will be able to tear away most of the paper, then spritz the quilt with water to dissolve the remaining small bits of stabilizer.

To run the stabilizer through an inkjet printer, you can either purchase precut stabilizer sheets (see Resources, page 126) or cut the stabilizer yourself to fit your printer. If the stabilizer passes the "stand at attention test"—it stands up straight as a regular piece of paper does when you hold it with a small cupping motion—then you can feed it into your printer as is. If it flops over or droops, you can try to iron it to a piece of freezer paper to stabilize it. However, I recommend that you stick to using stabilizer that is stiff enough to just run through your printer.

If you are using a wash-away stabilizer, keep the stroke weight of your lines to 1 point, and print using the Draft or Normal setting. Photo or Best quality will deposit too much ink, dissolving the stabilizer prematurely.

tip When buying precut stabilizer sheets, you may need to buy the size closest to what will fit your printer and either trim them down or adjust the page size.

PRINTING ON FREEZER PAPER

One last alternative is to print on the paper side of freezer paper and use an iron to tack these sheets directly to the quilt top. The benefit is that the plastic of the freezer paper allows you to have the design completely fastened down to the quilt top so that it doesn't move when you stitch, yet the pieces of paper can be removed when stitching is done.

One drawback to using freezer paper is that it can be harder to tear away because it's a little heavier paper and small pieces of the freezer paper can be left under stitches that have to be tweezed out. Also, some freezer paper contains more plastic than others, and a slight residue of plastic can be felt on the quilt top after removal if the freezer paper is left on the quilt top for an extended length of time. I recommend applying the freezer paper just to sections that you can complete and remove within a week or so.

HOW TO PRINT

To print a pattern that fits on one page, simply print as many copies of the page as you need. If you are printing a repeat/pantograph, use the top and side registration repeats (in this example shown in blue and gray) to align the pages and tape them together. Note that what you see beyond the rectangle of the printable page will not print. The lines that are cut off are for placement only and are not needed.

Print area

If you have a pattern that is larger than your paper, you can print it one portion at a time and tape the pages together. Your printer may have a tiling function that will automatically print all the pages you need with some overlap. This is something worth exploring in your printer software. It may be called *banner-style printing* or *poster printing* in some printer software.

When printing a pattern, remember to include the header and copyright information on at least one page that you print for the pattern.

If you are printing a pantograph or other long, thin design, you may be able to print it on continuous-feed paper (remember the old-style printer paper?) or on paper from a roll. Check to see how long a piece of paper your printer will print or look into software that prints banners.

Manually Dividing a Pattern for Printing

If your pattern takes up more than one page and your printer will not tile it for you, you need to move the pattern around in the graphic design program and print it a portion at a time.

In this situation, the printer will print only what is within the page outline in the graphic design program. If you are able to print on different sizes of paper, make sure the design page size is the same as the paper size. This is usually done by accessing the Document Setup menu item. In the following example, the paper size is 8½″ × 11″.

1. Start by positioning the upper left corner of the design within the page outline and within the margins. Print this page.

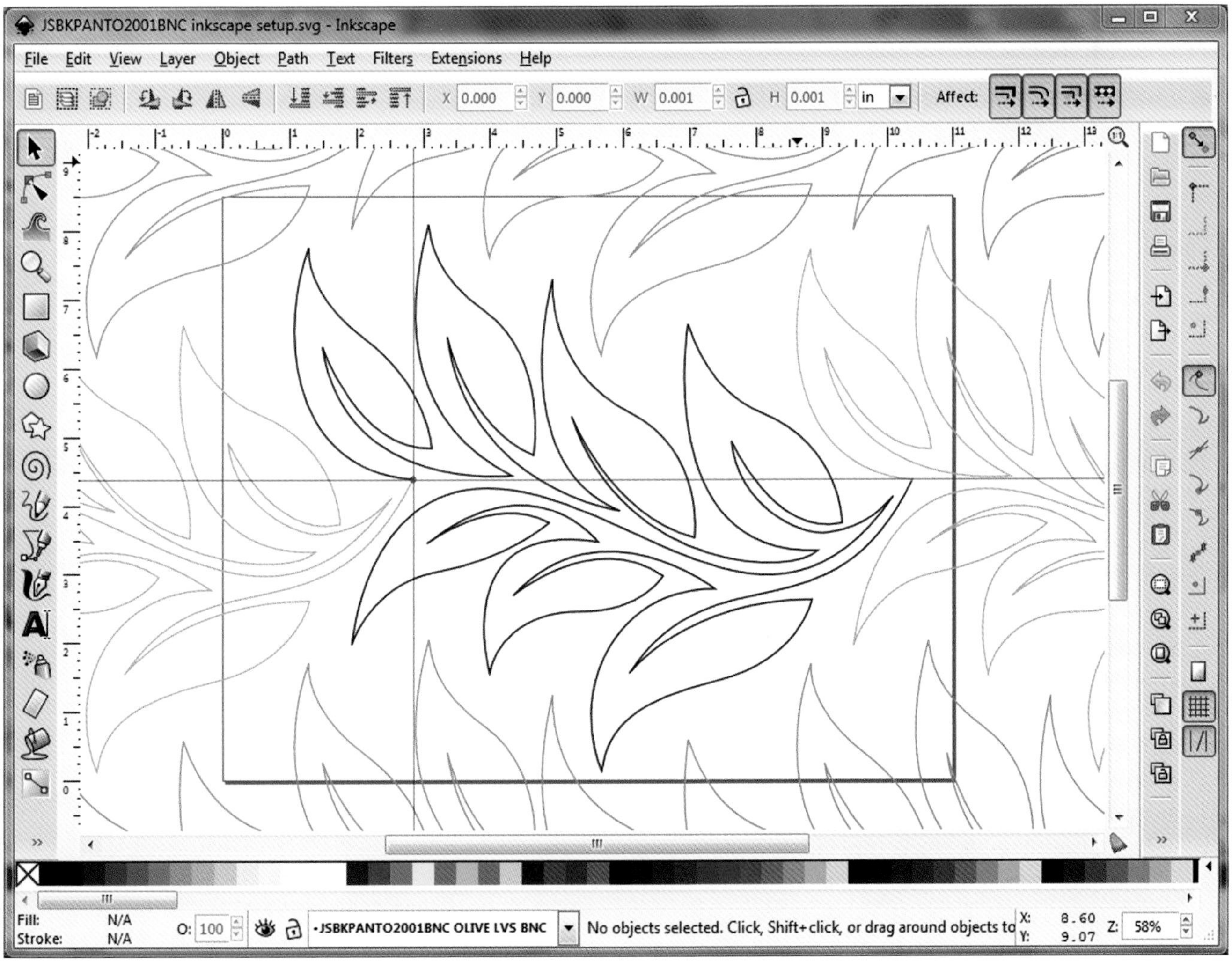

Position design in upper left corner of page outline.

2. Move the pattern by changing the numbers in the X and Y boxes in the top toolbar; for example, change the number in the X box to –7 (7″ to the left), giving yourself 1″ of overlap in printing on the sides to match up the pages.

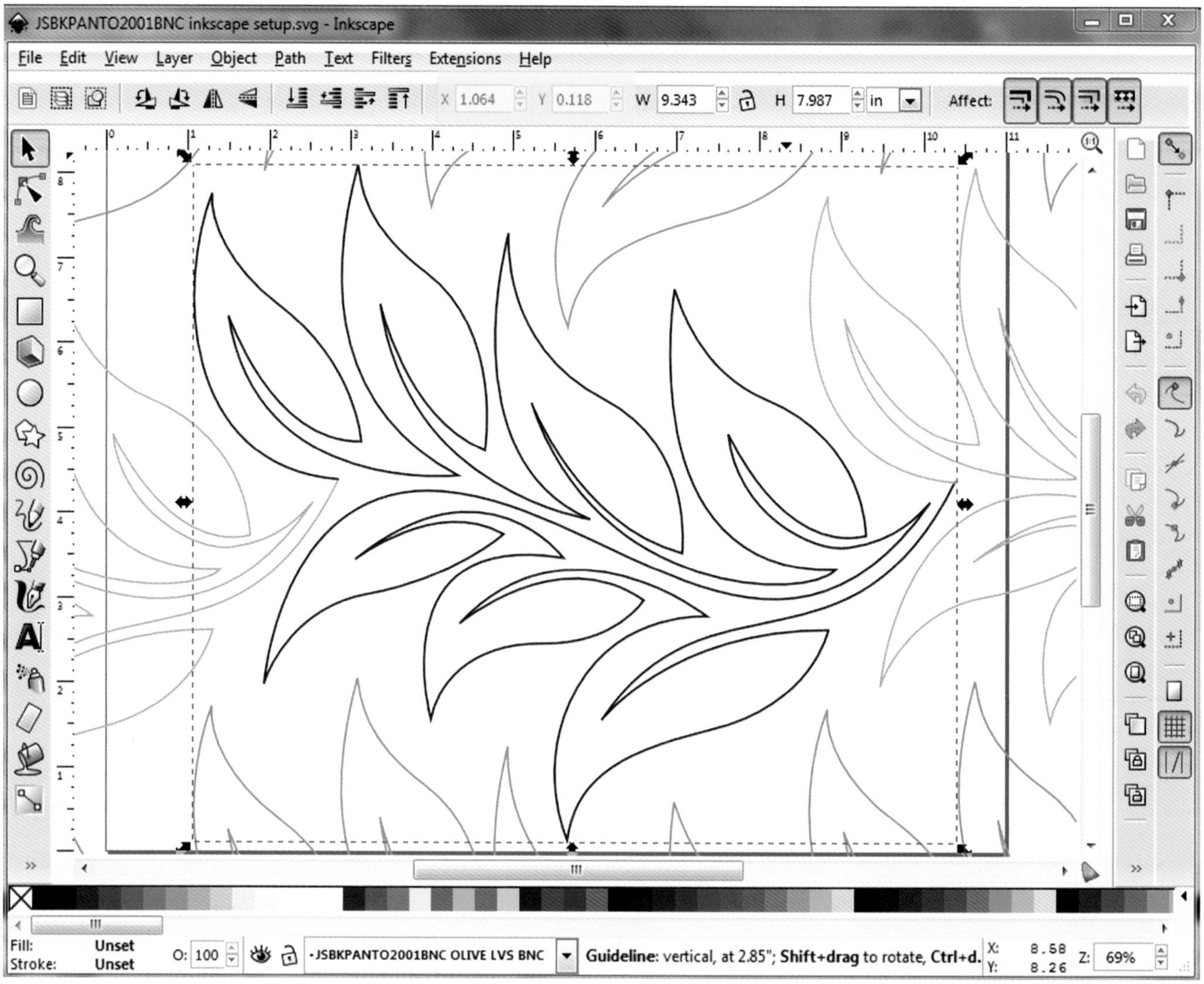

Use X and Y boxes to move design.

3. Continue moving the pattern to the left by increasing X by –7 each time, for example –14, –21, and so on.

4. If your pattern is bigger than about 10″ tall, you'll need to move the pattern up 10″ using the Y box and repeat the process.

5. Continue moving the pattern until you have printed out all the sections.

tip If you are planning on tracing the design onto your quilt top, before you print all the pages, test one page of the pattern to make sure you can see it clearly enough through the fabric to trace. If the lines are too faint, increase the stroke point size (see More Editing Options, page 20) and try again.

Using the Design Patterns

For hand quilting or hand-guided/free-motion quilting, now that you have your patterns printed or copied, you can use the patterns in several different ways:

- Trace the patterns onto the quilt top.
- Copy or trace the pattern onto an interfacing or thin paper and stitch through the printing (see Quilting, Part One: Hand Quilting and Domestic, Midarm, and Longarm Machines, page 26).
- Use the patterns with a pointer system on a longarm machine (see Quilting, Part Two: Computerized Longarm and Embroidery Machines, page 28).

Tracing Designs onto the Quilt Top

When you are going to trace the designs directly onto the quilt top, do so before you make the quilt sandwich and stabilize the quilt (see Stabilizing the Quilt, page 26).

MARKING TOOLS

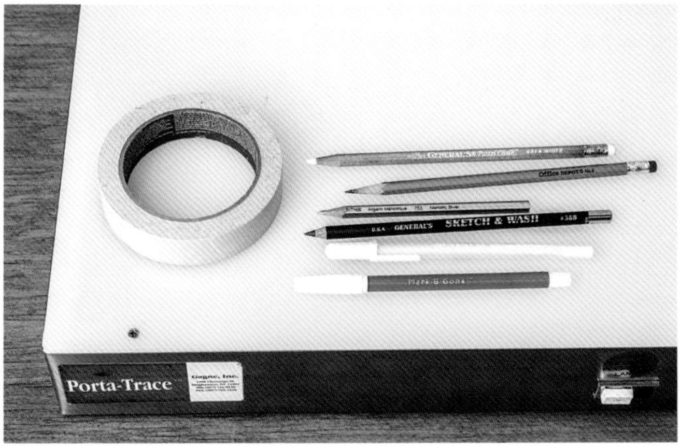

Marking tools

Several types of marking tools are available to use, depending on the fabrics in the quilt.

Wash-Away Marker

Wash-away markers are designed to stay visible until you wash away the marks. Test your marker—some do not wash out as easily as others. If you are considering using an air-erase marker, you have to make sure you complete the quilting before the lines disappear.

Graphite Pencils

As an option when marking light-colored fabrics, try a number 2, 2b, or 3b pencil. Graphite pencil washes out with the first wash. If the line is thin enough and I quilt right on top of the line, I can rarely see that it's there. This is a good option if the piece is something that you don't want to wash.

Sketch & Wash

A great pencil from General Pencil Company is Sketch & Wash. It has soft lead, so the marks are dark enough to see but they wash out easily. If any residual pencil lines do not come out with the first wash, I recommend using Kiss-Off Stain Remover. It is easy to apply and blot off, taking the pencil marks with it.

White Pens and Pencils

For working with dark fabrics, several options are available. I like the white gel pens from Gelly Roll because they glide onto the surface of the fabric and the marks come out with washing. Many white chalk pencils are very good, but my favorite is the white charcoal pencil by General Pencil Company. It goes on smoothly and stays on while I am quilting (the chalk from many chalk pencils bounces off). I can keep a sharp point on the General chalk pencil, and most importantly, brushing it off with a damp cloth removes it. I also like to use a silver Verithin Pencil, by Prismacolor, on any fabric where white or black markings wouldn't show. You can see the silver line on a fabric with a busy print.

> **tip** Another option for marking is a FriXion pen. It's a ballpoint pen, but the ink will disappear with friction. The heat of friction causes the ink to disappear, so the heat from ironing the fabric will also make any ink lines disappear. These pens come in a variety of colors. As with any marking tool, test it on scraps of each fabric in your quilt top to make sure the ink doesn't reappear when the fabrics cool.

LIGHTBOX

Using a lightbox when tracing makes the pattern easier to see. You can use a clear plastic bin turned upside down over a lamp as a makeshift lightbox. Along this same line, some people have a glass or clear plastic sewing machine extension table, and this works well with a light source underneath it. If your quilt top is not too large, you can also use a large window or a sliding glass door.

TAPE

To prevent movement, fasten the paper pattern with artist's or drafter's tape—it is like masking tape, but the tackiness of the glue is such that it easily comes off the surface without damaging it. Blue painter's tape also works well, since it is made to come off surfaces without leaving residue.

After you fasten down the pattern, fasten down the quilt top. This will prevent shifting during the tracing process. Use the same tape for this layer. Trace your designs, moving the fabric and retaping as needed.

> **tip** If you are tracing your designs onto lightweight interfacing, use the same process as if tracing onto the quilt top.

QUILTING, PART ONE: Hand Quilting and Domestic, Midarm, and Longarm Machines

STABILIZING THE QUILT

Whether you are quilting by hand, doing machine hand-guided / free-motion quilting, or using a computer-guided machine, you need to stabilize the quilt. Stabilizing helps prevent fabric from drawing up (see Fabric Draw-Up, next page) and can be used to define or outline areas for quilting.

Basting

For hand quilting and domestic or midarm quilting, you need to baste to hold together the three layers of the quilt (quilt top, batting, and backing). This is the first level of stabilizing a quilt. Thread basting is most traditional, pin basting usually works just fine, and some people use spray basting. With longarm quilting, the three layers are not held together prior to quilting because of the way they are loaded onto the machine. The details of basting are covered in Stabilizing Stitches (next page).

Stitching In-the-Ditch

The main job of stabilizing is done by stitching in-the-ditch (or something similar). This is easy and obvious when working on a pieced quilt. When working on non-traditional and wholecloth quilts, some type of stitching is also needed to stabilize the quilting surface. Having the quilt stabilized minimizes fabric shifting as you quilt. As I write, I have visions of how much I used to detest working with sashing and how it shifted if I didn't stitch in-the-ditch around every piece.

> **note** **FABRIC DRAW-UP** ■ As you quilt, the fabric draws in because the top and bottom threads interlock. In the process, the sewing pulls some of the top fabric and some of the backing fabric into the stitching groove. The fabric draws up more in the most heavily stitched areas compared with the areas that have less stitching. Stabilizing a quilt with stitching helps to equalize the fabric draw-up.

Using Interfacing as a Stabilizer

Interfacing can be used as a stabilizer in unique situations. If the design pattern is particularly dense or if it is so large that you have to split the design to get it to fit by advancing the quilt on a longarm machine, then put a layer of very lightweight interfacing, or stabilizer meant for embroidery, between the batting and the quilt top before quilting. The lightweight interfacing can remain between the quilt layers without a problem. In fact, in a wallhanging, the interfacing does a particularly good job of keeping the fabric from being wobbly. However, if the quilt is a bed-size quilt, I suggest using wash-away stabilizer.

Stabilizing Stitches

Stitch in-the-ditch stabilizing is meant to stay in the quilt. Other types of stabilizing stitches are meant to be temporary. For temporary stitching—

- Use vanishing or wash-away thread in either the bobbin or the top. That way, when you soak the quilt for blocking, the thread washes away and the remaining thread is easy to remove.
- Use a thread that matches the background fabric. This way, if you don't get it all out, then it's not noticeable.

Regardless of how you are stitching to stabilize, I suggest you start in the middle of the quilt and stitch toward the outside. This way if the fabric draws up when you quilt, it will be relatively equal in all directions. Mark the center with a pin, a crease, or a marking tool, and work out from there.

For more details on stabilizing when using computer-guided quilting, see Quilting, Part Two: Computerized Longarm and Embroidery Machines (page 28).

QUILTING

If you traced or drew the design on the quilt top, quilt as usual.

If you are quilting through a printed pattern (on paper or stabilizer), you can attach the patterns to the quilt sandwich in any of several ways:

- **Pins, glue dots, tape** For small areas, you can pin the pattern in the corners and in a few places inside the design, preferably where you won't be stitching. You may also be able to use glue dots or tape. Try them out on a test piece of fabric and see if they hold well enough and remove cleanly.
- **Temporary spray basting** This product evaporates after a few hours, so plan your quilting accordingly.
- **Regular light spray adhesive** If temporary spray basting is not available, you can use regular fabric spray adhesive. I recommend spraying the paper or stabilizer lightly, pressing it to a somewhat fuzzy or linty fabric to reduce the tackiness a little bit, and then sticking it onto the quilt top for stitching.

> **note** If you are going to stitch through a printed pattern as opposed to tracing the pattern directly onto the quit top, you should know that some printer inks will transfer through the stitching. To help avoid this, make sure the ink is completely dry before stitching; you can even iron it to make sure the ink is dry. Before stitching your project, stitch on practice fabric to resolve any ink issues. You may be able to use an ink color similar to the quilt top or thread color if there are ink problems.

When you are done with the quilting, if you stitched through paper or stabilizer, remove it based on the type of paper or stabilizer used.

QUILTING, PART TWO:
Computerized Longarm and Embroidery Machines

This part covers both computerized longarm and embroidery machines because the process is similar for both machine types. After all, when you add a computerized system to your longarm, you essentially have created a machine that stitches in a very large hoop (your quilting frame).

Those of you who have a computerized quilting system already know how to use digital patterns. Let's focus on dividing up your quilting spaces, picking design patterns, and getting the patterns exactly where you want them.

SOFTWARE

Many computerized quilting and embroidery systems have software that will allow you to do an entire quilt or block layout on your machine. That's great. But for those who do not have that feature on your system, you can use the same computer graphics programs described in Customizing Design Patterns (page 10).

PREPARATION

Follow the same preparation as for all other types of quilting:

- Analyze and break up the area of the quilt top as needed to work with your selected patterns (Planning Your Quilting, page 7).
- Customize the patterns as needed (Customizing Design Patterns, page 10).
- Check the patterns for scale (page 21).
- And yes, you need to stabilize the quilt even with computer-guided quilting. For the basics of stabilizing, see Stabilizing the Quilt (page 26).

tip When using a computer-guided quilting machine, see if your system will baste an outline of the programmed quilting blocks or areas. If it does, not only can you use this basting to stabilize your quilts, but it will also help you visualize the final product before doing all the quilting.

USING AN EMBROIDERY MACHINE TO QUILT

Using an embroidery machine to quilt is a technique I've been waiting for years to become more popular. It's a great way for those quilters who don't have the space or just don't want to go the longarm route to quilt with the precision of computerized quilting systems.

The embroidery machines with larger hoops are great for this, but don't feel like you have to have the jumbo hoops. You will just have to hoop multiple times if you have limited hooping options.

I recommend stabilizing the quilt sandwich, either by stitching in-the-ditch (page 26) with any sewing machine or by pin basting. The advantage of stitching in-the-ditch is that you won't have to remove pins as you hoop. You may still need to pin a bit here and there around the main block or segments of your quilt, but you won't need to go around every piece of fabric that's been used in the piecing.

You may not have to use additional stabilizer when quilting on the embroidery machine. I don't have a problem with this most of the time. If you do a test first and find that you have a lot of fabric draw-up (page 27) or shifting, you can stabilize from the inside out by putting a piece of wash-away or soft cut-away stabilizer between the batting and the quilt top. If you use a lightweight cut-away stabilizer, you may not even be able to feel that it's there when you are done, and it will soften up after the first washing. I like to use a very lightweight interfacing material for this purpose when needed. However, my favorite is a wash-away stabilizer from Baby Lock. Many brands of wash-away stabilizer are available that work just as well.

Design Suite of Patterns on CD

The design suites on the included CD are a collection of design patterns to be used together or independently. All the designs are identified in the book with PDF numbers, which are on the CD in a PDF folder for each suite.

Some design patterns in the book are available in the following formats to be used as described. If the designs are noted to have these additional file formats for embroidery and quilting, use the long stock number (such as JSBK5000) to locate the design on the CD in the quilting and embroidery suite folders. Some design patterns will have arrows indicating the stitching direction.

Also on the CD is a gallery of quilts, using the designs from this book.

Artwork Files for Modifying and Printing

PDF Vector artwork files can be used to download, resize, and print from your own printer or at local print shop; see How to Use This Book (page 6), Customizing Design Patterns (page 10), and Using the Design Patterns (page 25).

Computer-Assisted Quilting Formats

CQP CompuQuilter and Quilt Path

DXF Most computerized quilting systems are able to use DXF, or a new format may be written from this type. Please see your manual to find out if your quilting software will read this file format directly.

GPF Quilt Artist, QuiltCAD, Quilter's Creative Touch, Quilt*magine*, QuiltMotion, Quilt Path, QuiltSewClever

HQF Handi Quilter, Pro-Stitcher

IQP IntelliQuilter

PAT Innova AutoPilot

PLT QBOT (also reads 4QB)

QLI CompuQuilter, Pro-Stitcher, Shirley Stitcher, Statler Stitcher, Quilt Artist, Quilt Magician, QuiltMotion, Quilt Path, QuiltSewClever

SSD Side Saddle system

TXT HQ Pro-Stitcher, PC Quilter

Embroidery Formats

CSD, DST, EXP, HUS, JEF, JEF+, PES, SEW, SHV, VIP, VP3, XXX

We have included several sizes for many of the patterns. You will need to determine what size your specific embroidery machine will accept. The required hoop size for each design is shown in the title of the file. Refer to your machine manual as needed.

Layout idea

JSBK1001 Baroque Floral Block 1

JSBK1001V1 Baroque Floral Continuous Triangle 1

JSBK1001V2 Baroque Floral Block 2

JSBK1001V3 Baroque Floral Block 3

JSBK1002 Baroque Floral Block 4

JSBK1003 Baroque Floral Block 7

JSBK1004 Baroque Angels OP Block

JSBK1011 Baroque Angels Border Element

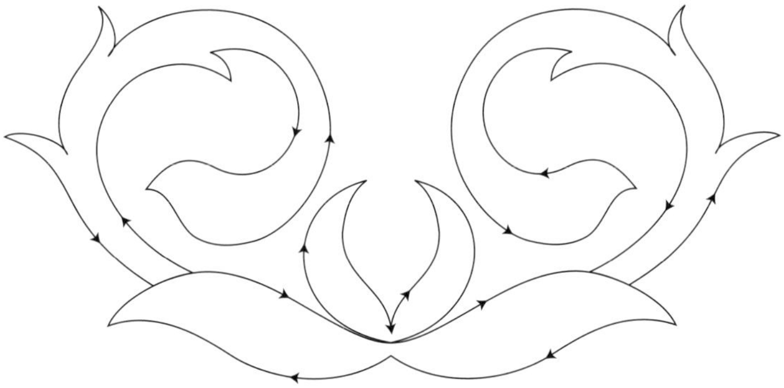

JSBK1005 Baroque Floral Block

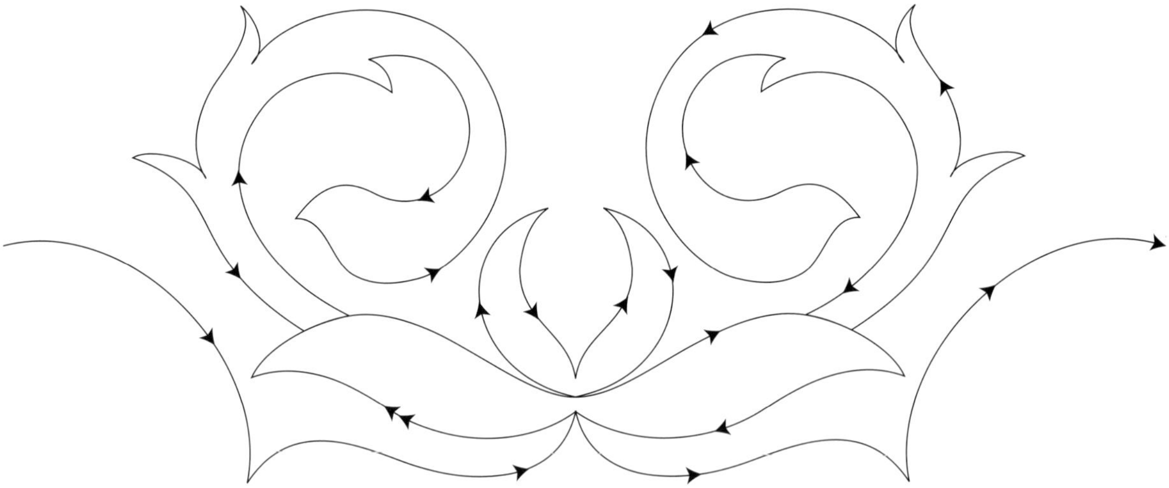

JSBK1006 Baroque Angels P2P Element

Layout idea

Layout ideas

JSBK1007 Baroque Angels Block

JSBK1008 Baroque Angels Block

JSBK1002V2 Baroque Floral Block 6
(Available on the CD in computer-assisted quilting and embroidery formats)

Layout idea

JSBK1009 Baroque Angels Triangle

JSBKPANTO1001BNC Baroque Angels Border & Corner

JSBK1009V1 Baroque Angels Continuous Triangle
(Available on the CD in computer-assisted quilting and embroidery formats)

JSBKPANTO1003A Baroque Leaves 2 Panto

JSBK1002V1 Baroque Floral Block 5

Layout ideas

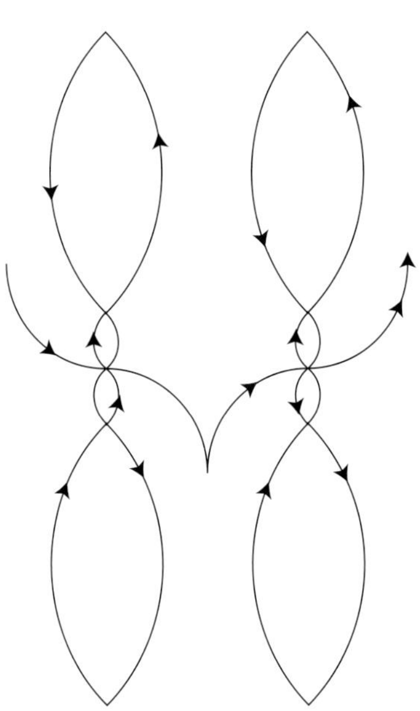

JSBKPANTO1004 Baroque Simple E2E Panto

JSBK1010 Baroque Angels Frame

Layout idea

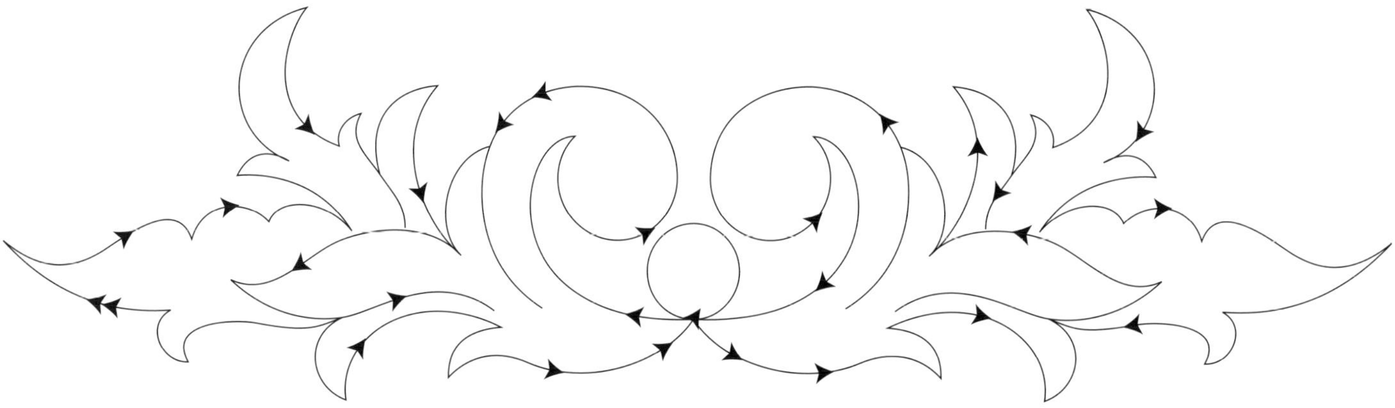

JSBK1011 Baroque Angels Border Element
(Available on the CD in computer-assisted quilting and embroidery formats)

Layout idea

JSBK1012 Baroque Angels Continuous Triangle
(Available on the CD in computer-assisted quilting and embroidery formats)

Layout ideas

Layout ideas

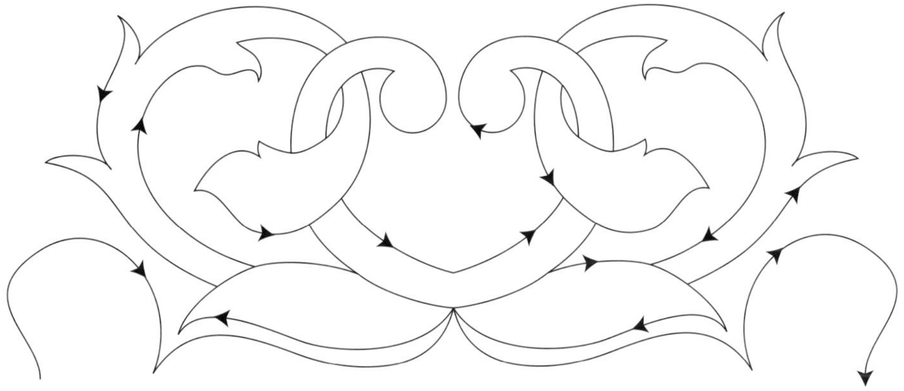

JSBKPANTO1003 Baroque Leaves 2 Panto

Layout idea

JSBKPANTO1002 Baroque Leaves E2E Panto
(Available on the CD in computer-assisted quilting and embroidery formats)

SUITE 2: *Olive Leaves*

Layout idea

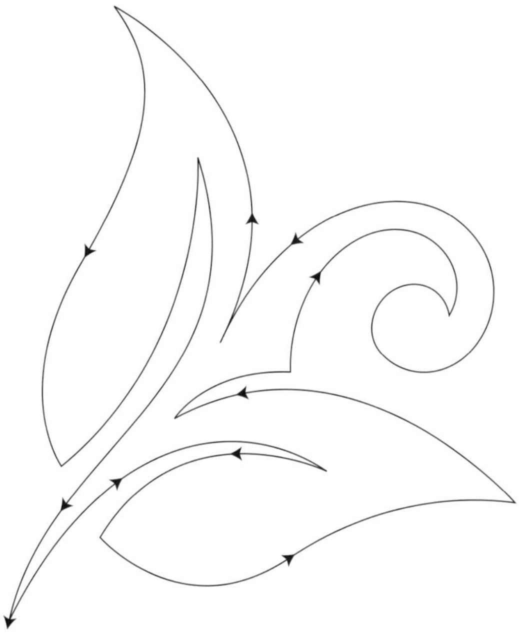

JSBK2001 Olive Leaves Element
(Available on the CD in computer-assisted quilting and embroidery formats)

JSBK2001V1 Olive Leaves Block

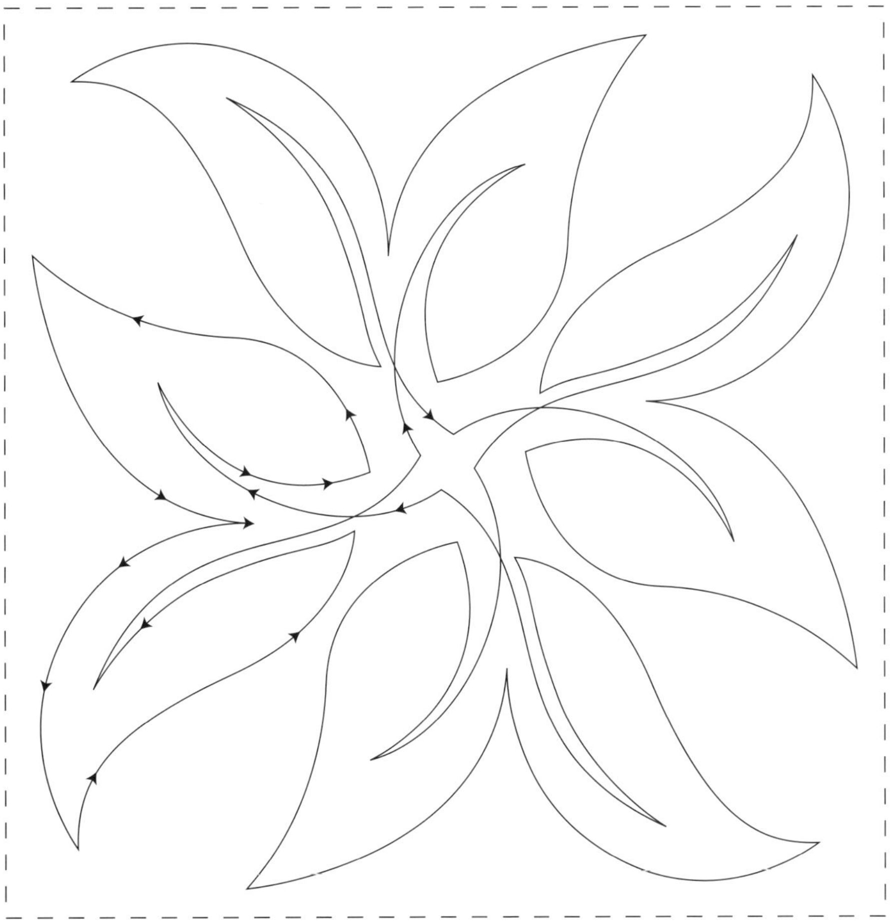

JSBK2001V2 Olive Leaves Block

JSBK2002 Olive Leaves Circle Block

JSBK2002V1 Olive Leaves Wreath

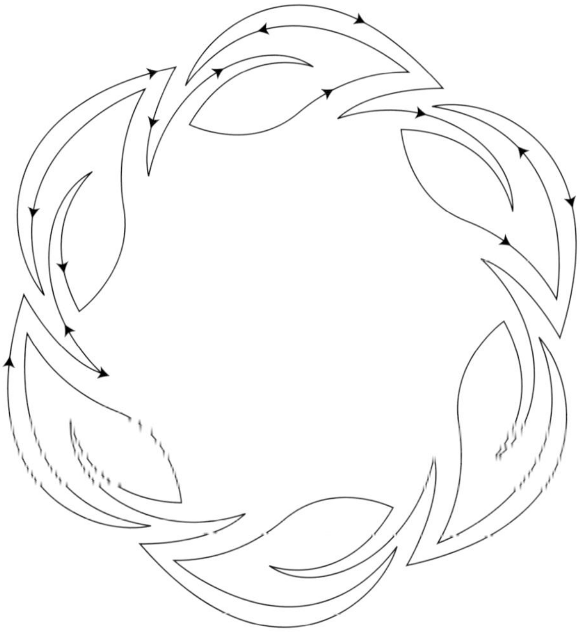

JSBK2002V2 Olive Leaves Wreath

JSBK2003 Olive Leaves Element
(Available on the CD in computer-assisted quilting and embroidery formats)

JSBK2003V1 Olive Leaves Block

JSBK2003V2 Olive Leaves Block

Layout idea

JSBK2003V3 Olive Leaves Triangle
(Available on the CD in computer-assisted quilting and embroidery formats)

JSBK2003V4 Olive Leaves Block

Layout idea

Layout idea

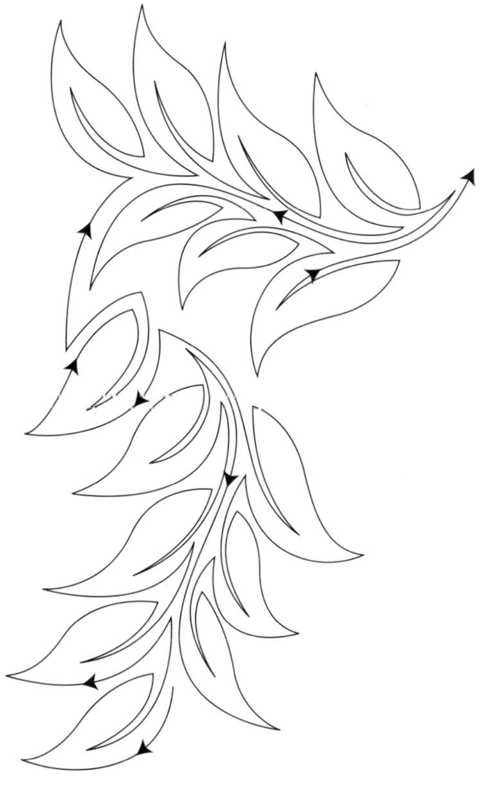

JSBKPANTO2001BNC Olive Leaves Border & Corner
(Available on the CD in computer-assisted quilting and embroidery formats)

Layout idea

SUITE 3: *Shaggy Leaves*

Layout idea

Layout idea

JSBK3001 Shaggy Leaves Block
(Available on the CD in computer-assisted quilting and embroidery formats)

JSBK3002 Shaggy Leaves Block

Layout idea

JSBK3003V1 Shaggy Leaves Frame

JSBK3002V1 Shaggy Leaves Block

Layout idea

JSBK3003 Shaggy Leaves Border Block

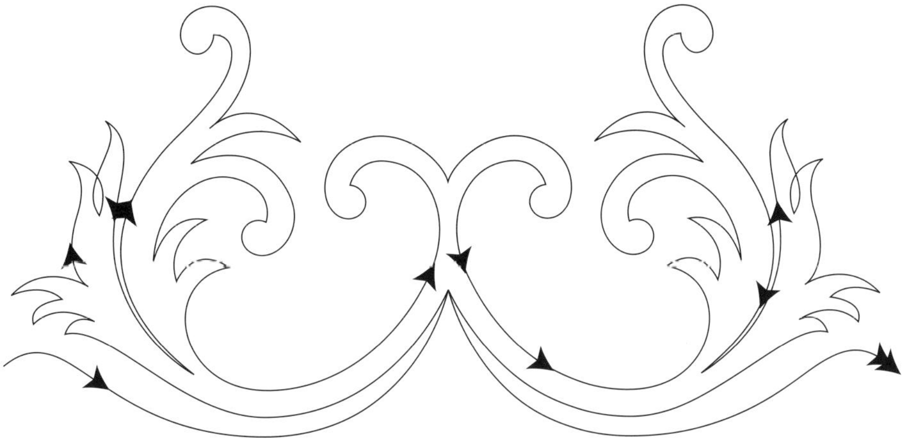

JSBKPANTO3001 Shaggy Leaves P2P Panto

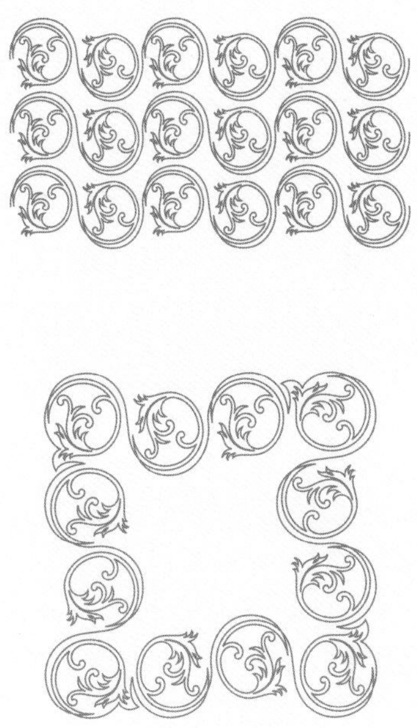

Layout ideas

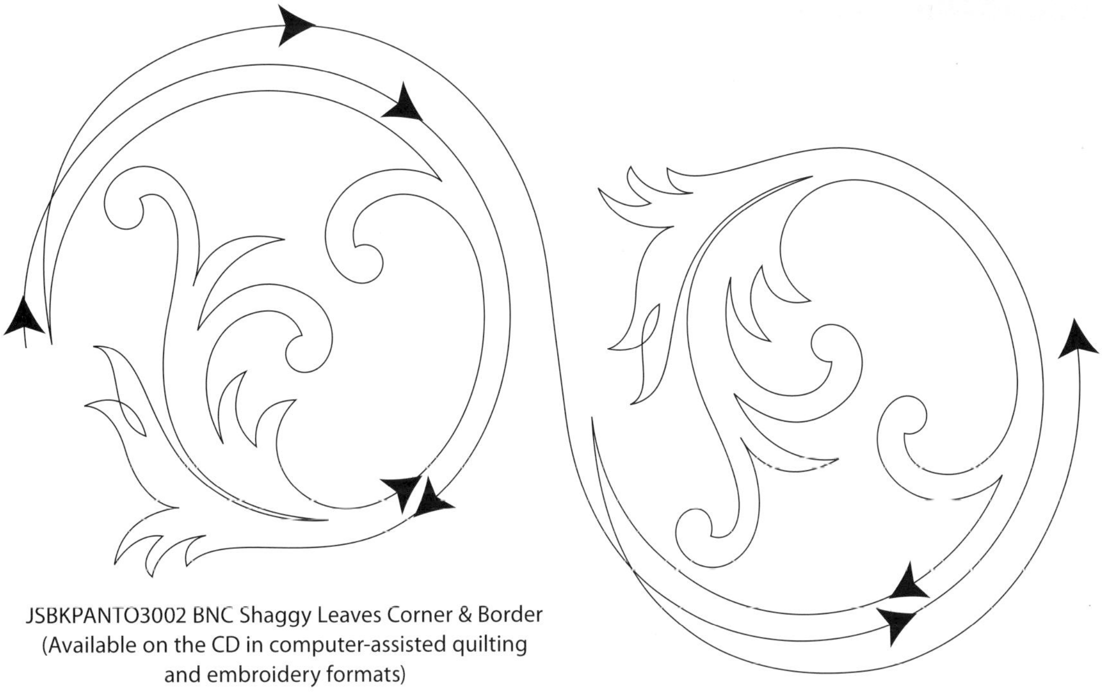

JSBKPANTO3002 BNC Shaggy Leaves Corner & Border
(Available on the CD in computer-assisted quilting
and embroidery formats)

SUITE 4: *Spades*

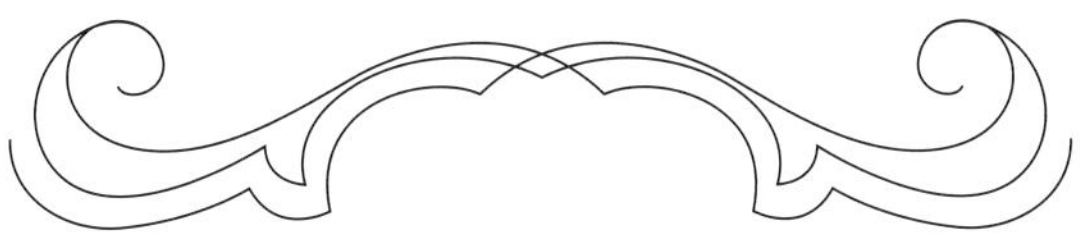

Layout idea

JSBK4000V1 Spades Block

JSBK4000V2 Spades Block

JSBK4002 Spades Block

JSBK4003V1 Spades Block

JSBK4004 Spades Frame

JSBK4004V1 Spades Frame 2

JSBK4004V2 Spades Frame

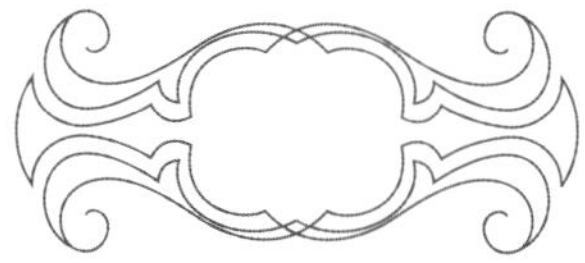

Spades Mini Frame alternate view

Layout idea

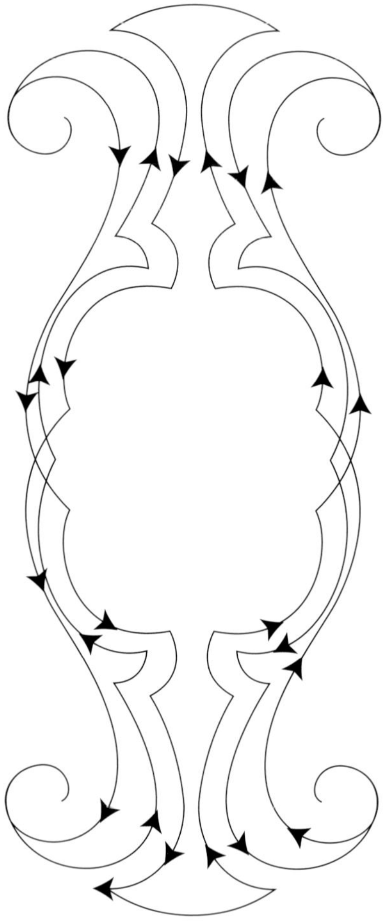

JSBK4005 Spades Mini Frame

JSBKPANTO4000 Spades Continuous Triangle Panto
(Available on the CD in computer-assisted quilting and embroidery formats)

Layout idea

JSBKPANTO4001 Spades Continuous Triangle Panto

Layout ideas

Layout ideas

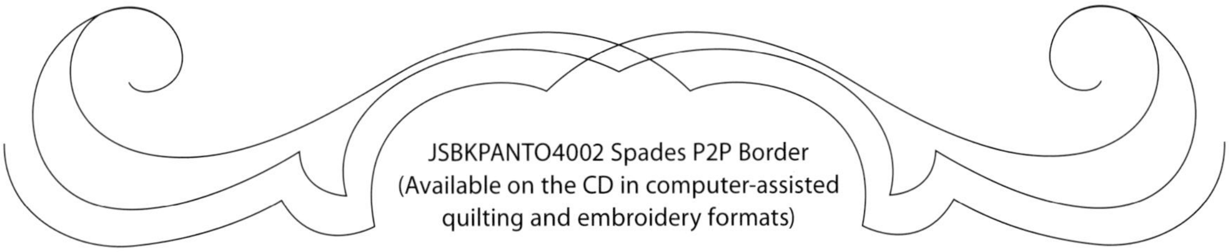

JSBKPANTO4002 Spades P2P Border
(Available on the CD in computer-assisted quilting and embroidery formats)

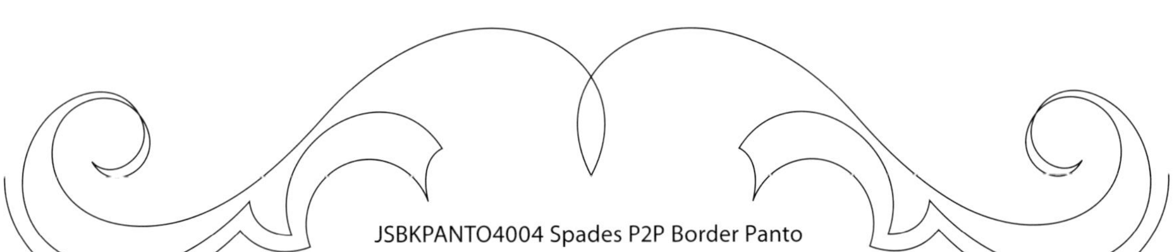

JSBKPANTO4004 Spades P2P Border Panto
(Available on the CD in computer-assisted quilting and embroidery formats)

SUITE 5: *Fleur-de-Lis*

Layout idea

Layout idea

JSBK5000 Fleur-de-Lis Element
(Available on the CD in computer-assisted quilting and embroidery formats)

JSBK5000V1 Fleur-de-Lis Block

JSBK5000V2 Fleur-de-Lis Block

JSBK5000V3 Fleur-de-Lis Block

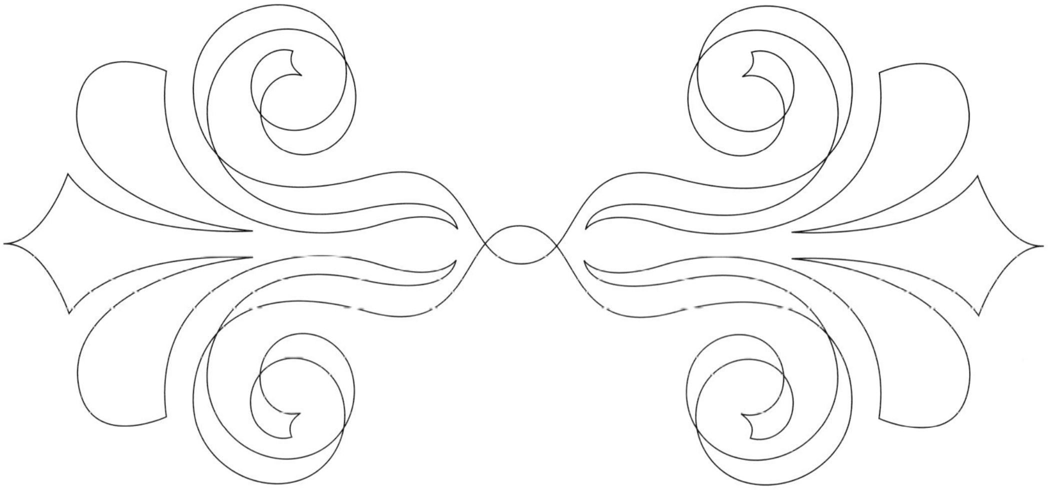

JSBK5001 Fleur-de-Lis Block
(Available on the CD in computer-assisted quilting and embroidery formats)

JSBK5001V1 Fleur-de-Lis Block

JSBK5001V2 Fleur-de-Lis Block

JSBK5001V3 Fleur-de-Lis Octagon

Layout idea

JSBK5001V4 Fleur-de-Lis Octagon 2

Layout ideas

JSBKPANTO5001BNC Fleur-de-Lis Corner & Border
(Available on the CD in computer-assisted quilting and embroidery formats)

Layout idea

JSBKPANTO5002 Fleur-de-Lis P2P Panto

SUITE 6: *Imperial Leaf*

Layout idea

JSBK6001 Imperial Diamond Block
(Available on the CD in computer-assisted quilting
and embroidery formats)

JSBK6003 Imperial Block
(Available on the CD in computer-assisted quilting
and embroidery formats)

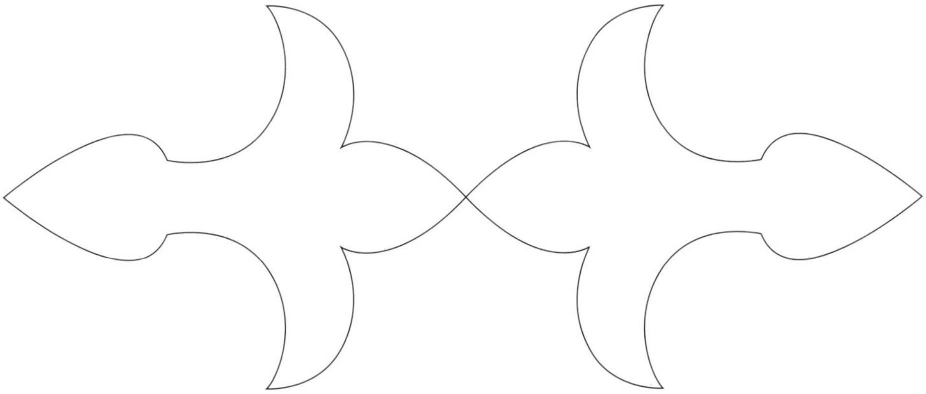

JSBK6002 Imperial Sashing Block
(Available on the CD in computer-assisted quilting
and embroidery formats)

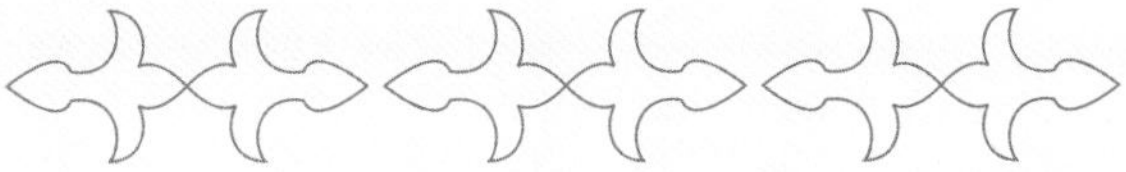

Layout idea

JSBK6004 Imperial Block

JSBK6005 Imperial Block

JSBK6006 Imperial Block

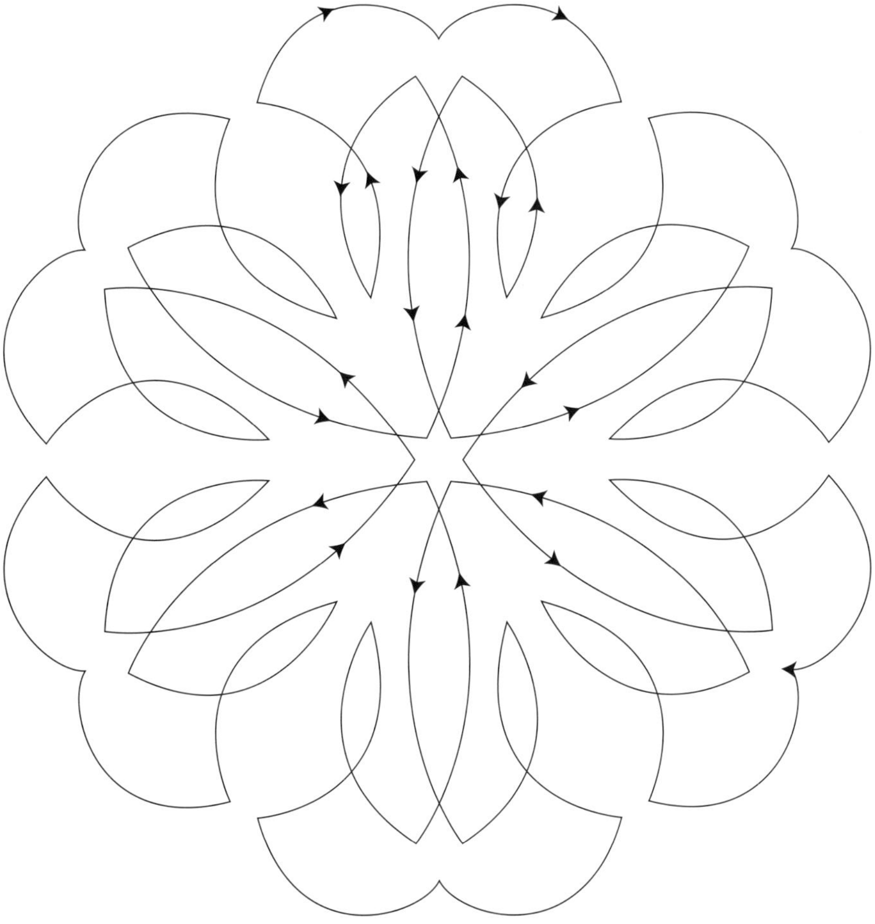

JSBK6007 Imperial Doily

Layout idea

JSBK6008 Imperial Circle Block

JSBK6009 Imperial Hexagon

JSBK6010 Imperial Kaleidoscope Star

Layout idea

JSBKPANTO601 Imperial E2E Panto

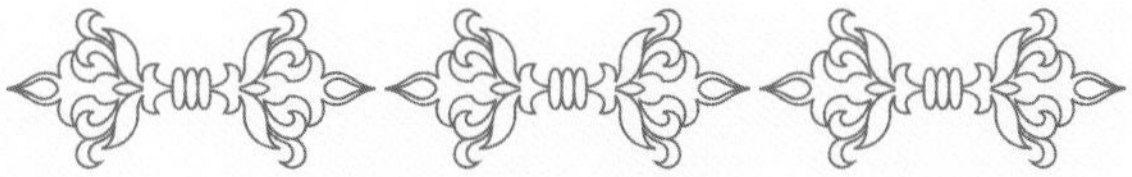

Layout idea

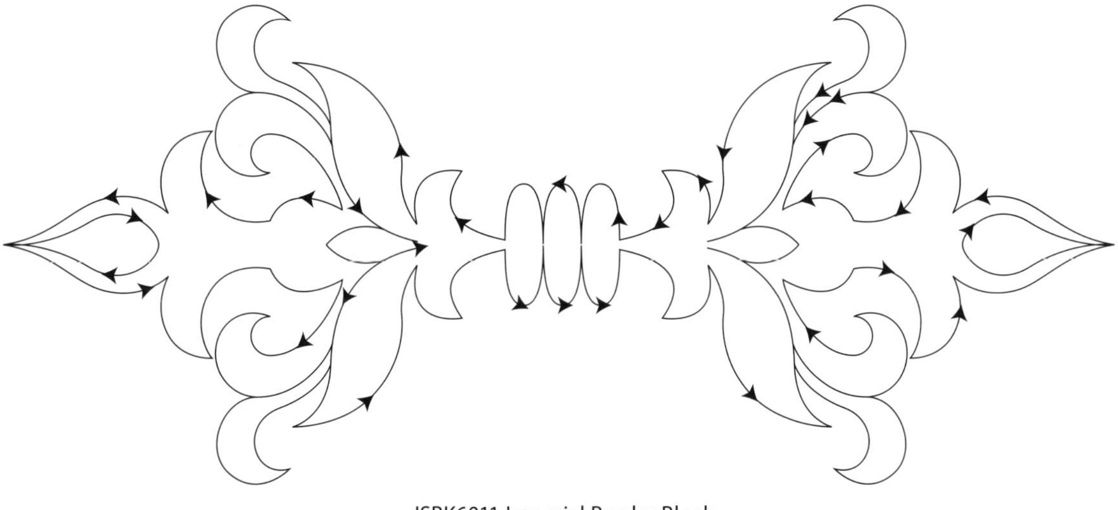

JSBK6011 Imperial Border Block

SUITE 7: *Byzantine Arches*

Layout idea

Layout idea

Layout idea

JSBK7000 Byzantine P2P Element

JSBK7001 Byzantine 8PT Block

JSBK7002 Byzantine Simple Block

JSBK7003 Byzantine Block

JSBK7004 Byzantine Block

JSBK7006 Byzantine Circle Motif

JSBK7005 Byzantine Double Wedding Ring Block & Melon

JSBK7008 Byzantine Frame

JSBK7009 Byzantine Circular Frame

JSBK7010 Byzantine Frame

JSBK7007 Byzantine Kaleidoscope Star

Layout idea

JSBK7011 Byzantine Runner

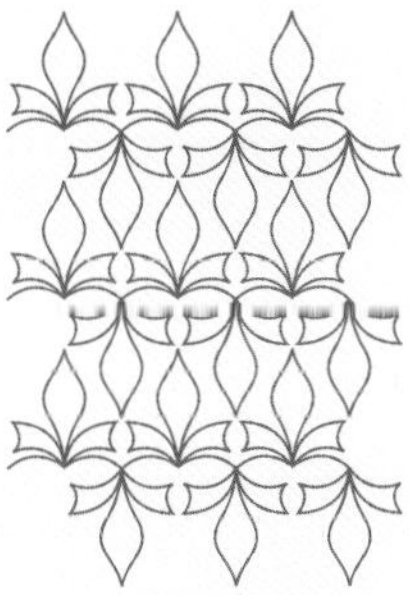

Layout idea

Layout idea

Layout idea

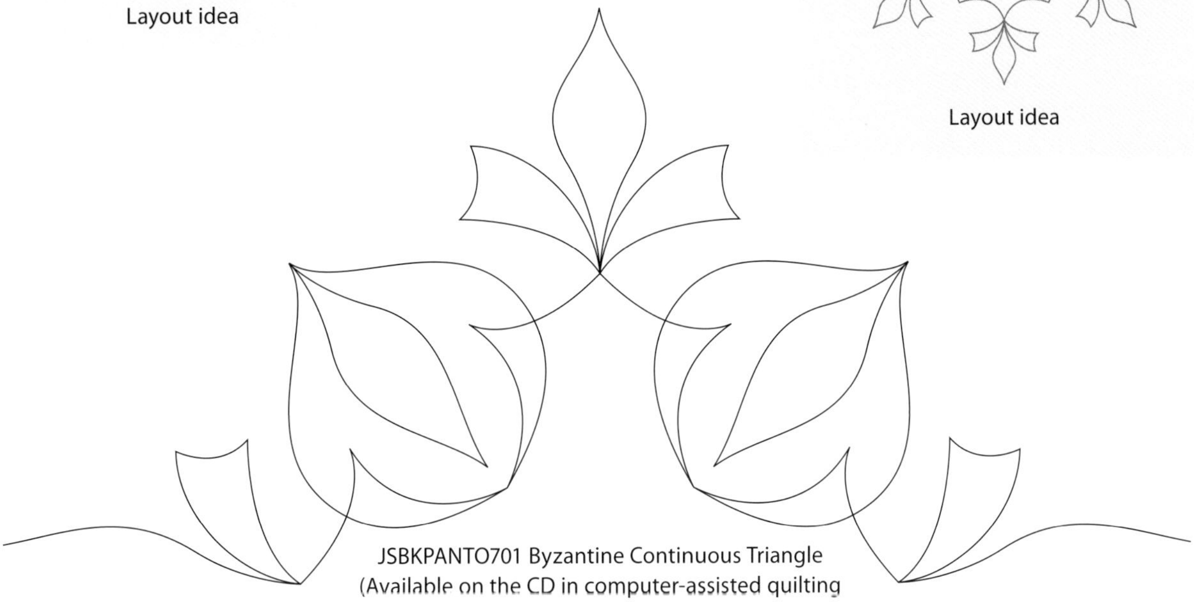

JSBKPANTO701 Byzantine Continuous Triangle
(Available on the CD in computer-assisted quilting
and embroidery formats)

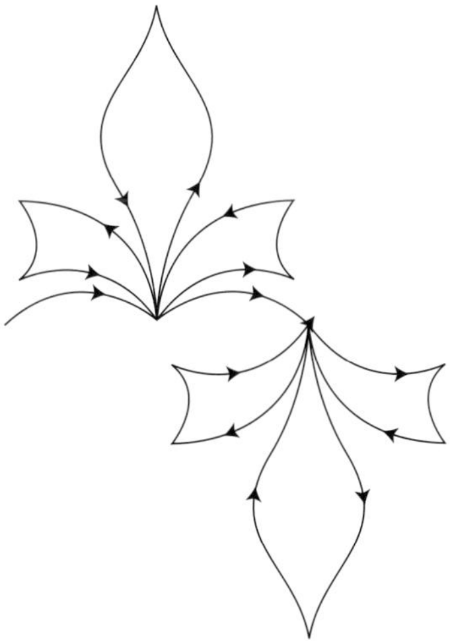

JSBKPANTO702 Byzantine Panto
(Available on the CD in computer-assisted quilting
and embroidery formats)

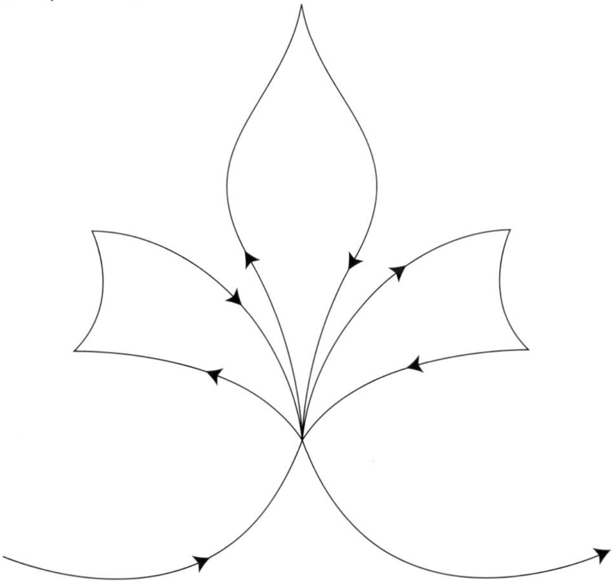

JSBKPANTO703 Byzantine P2P Panto 1

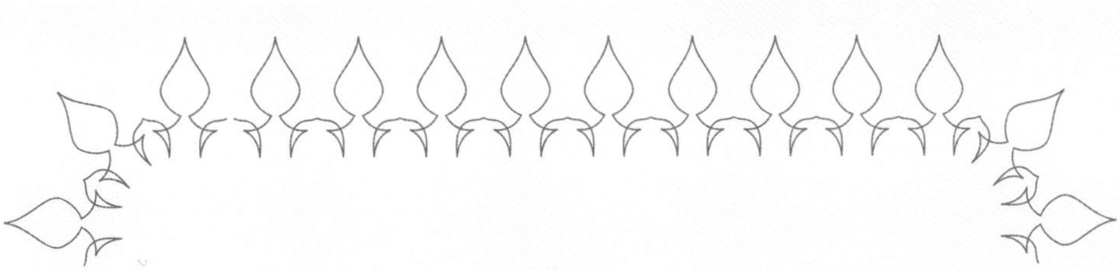

Layout idea

Corner created by rotating wedge pattern 45°

Layout idea

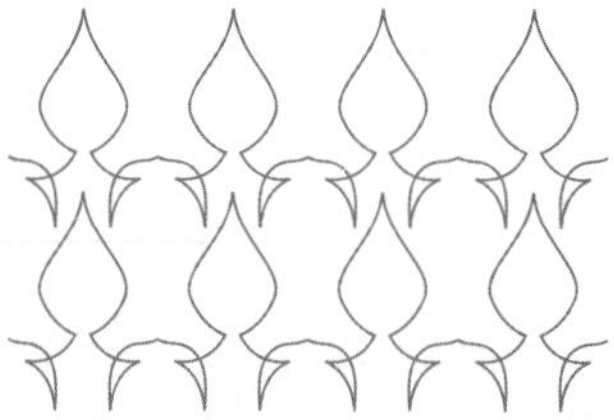

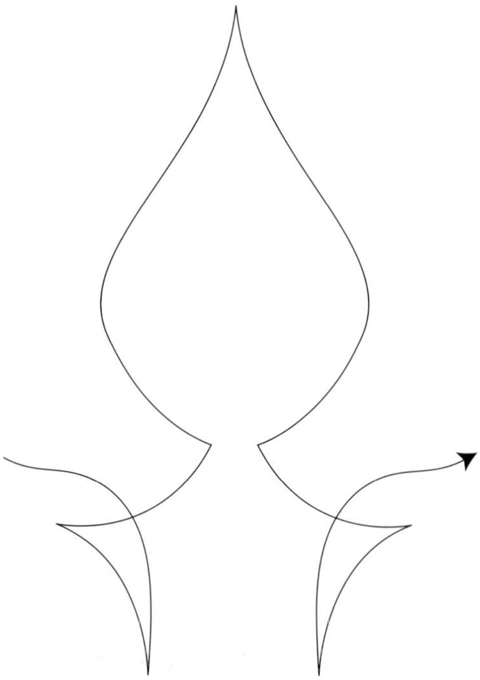

JSBKPANTO704 Byzantine P2P Wedge Panto
(Available on the CD in computer-assisted quilting and embroidery formats)

Layout ideas

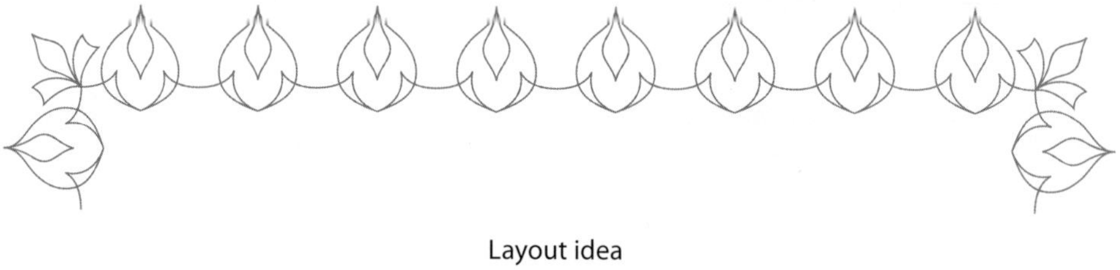

Layout idea

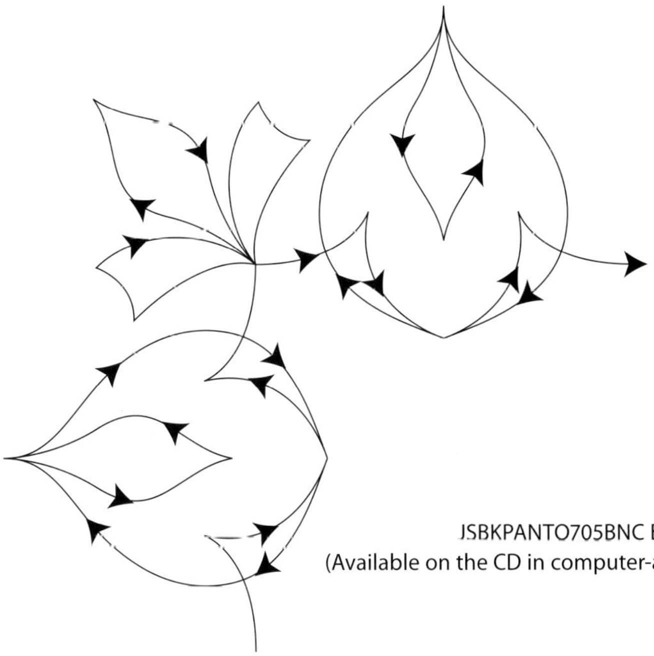

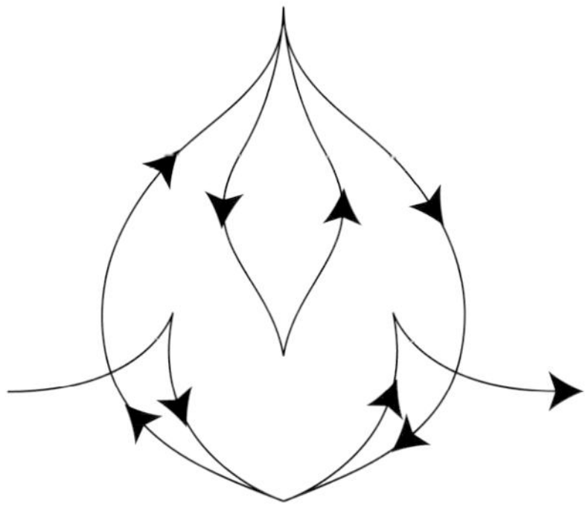

JSBKPANTO705BNC Byzantine Border & Corner 1
(Available on the CD in computer-assisted quilting and embroidery formats)

Layout idea

JSBKPANTO706BNC Byzantine Border & Corner 2

SUITE 8: *Simply Loopy Leaves*

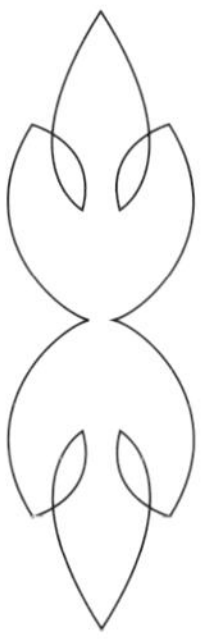
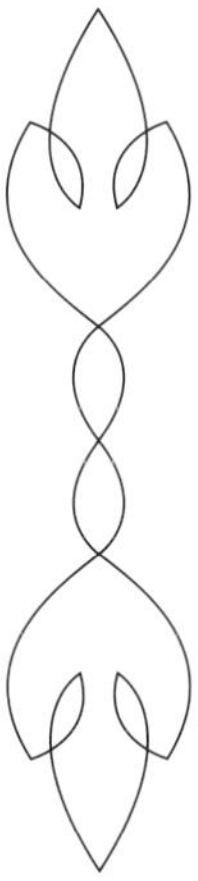

Layout idea

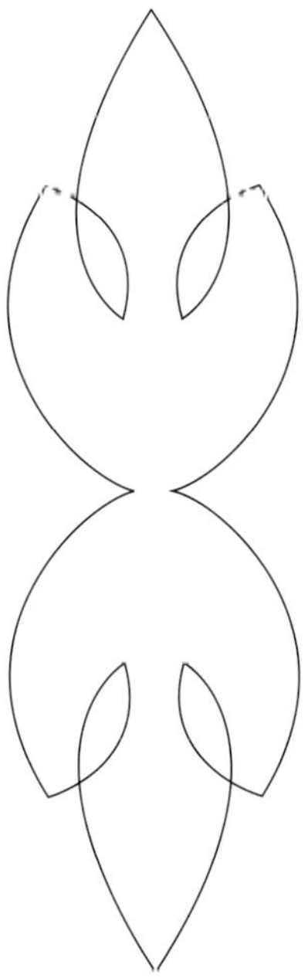

JSBK8000V2 Simple Leaf Sashing Block

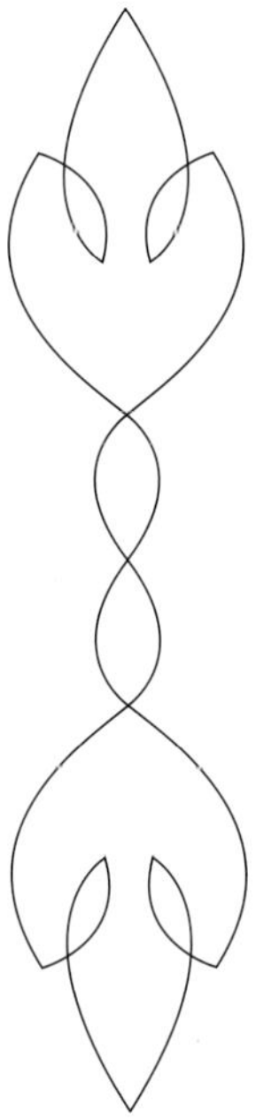

JSBK8000V3 Simple Leaf Sashing Block 2

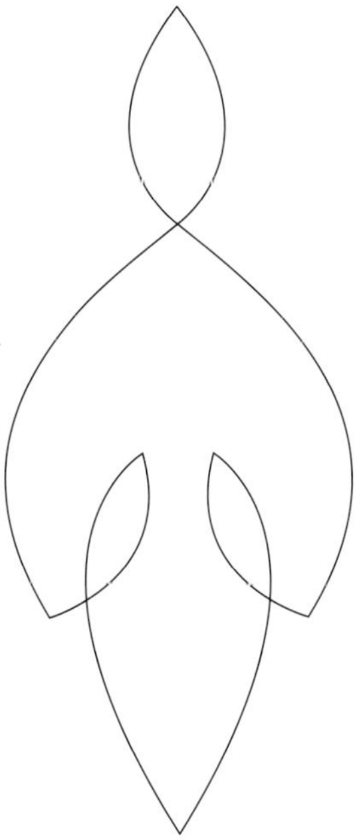

JSBK8000V1 Simple Leaf Element
(Available on the CD in computer-assisted quilting and embroidery formats)

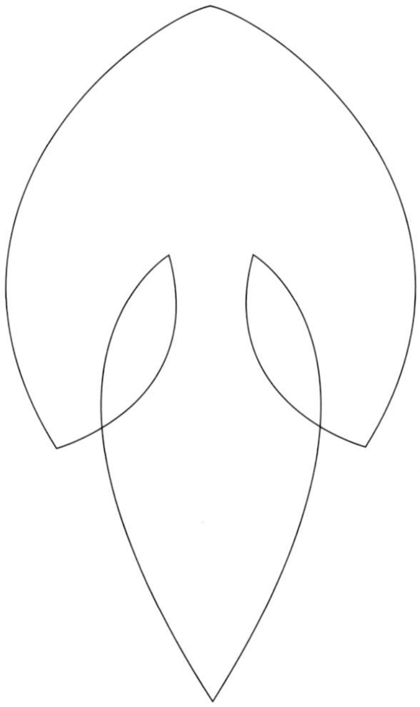

JSBK8000 Simple Leaf Element
(Available on the CD in computer-assisted quilting and embroidery formats)

JSBK8000V4 Simple Leaf Block

JSBK8000V5 Simple Leaf Block

JSBK8000V6 Simple Leaf Block

JSBK8000V7 Simple Leaf Star

Layout ideas

JSBK8001 Simple Leaf Continuous Triangle
(Available on the CD in computer-assisted quilting and embroidery formats)

JSBK8001V1 Simple Leaf Block

JSBK8001V2 Simple Leaf Block

JSBK8002 Simple Leaf Block

JSBK8003 Simple Leaf Block

Layout idea

JSBK8003V1 Simple Leaf Hexagon

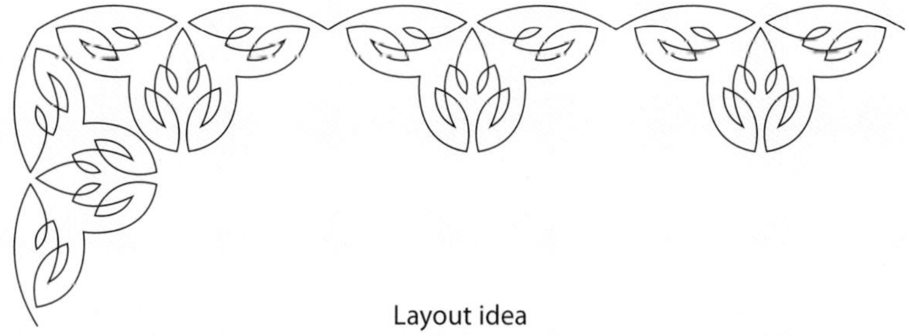

Layout idea

JSBKPANTO801 Simple Leaf Swag Continuous Triangle

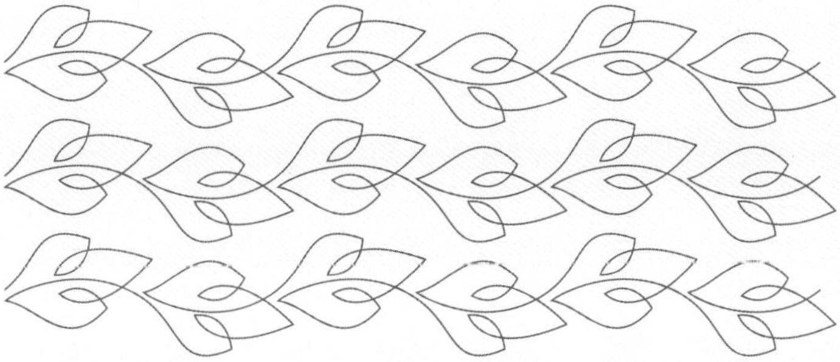

Layout idea

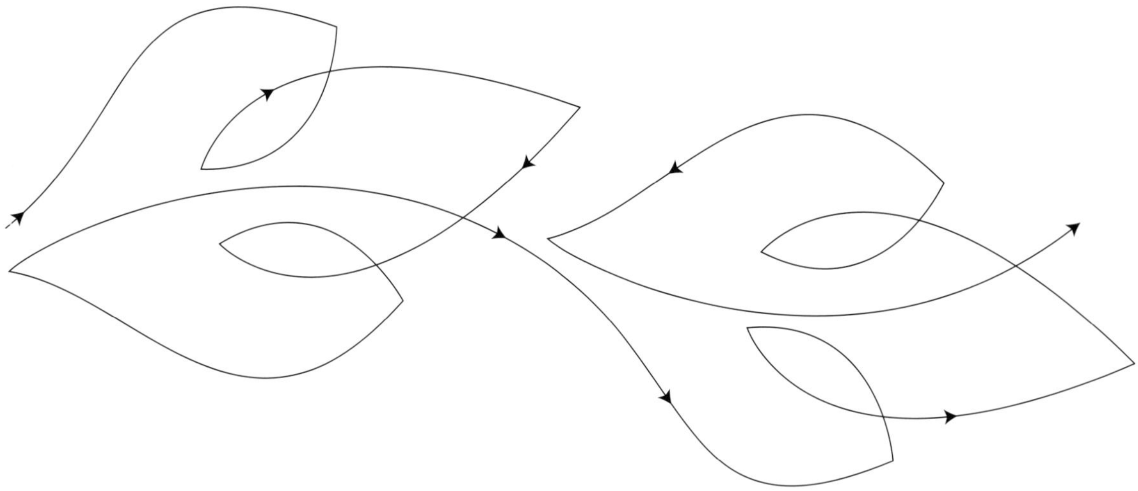

JSBKPANTO802 Simple Leaf Panto 1

Layout idea

Layout ideas

JSBKPANTO803BNC Simple Leaf Diagonal Border & Corner
(Available on the CD in computer-assisted quilting
and embroidery formats)

Layout idea

Layout idea

JSBKPANTO804BNC
Simple Leaf Large Corner & Leaf
(Available on the CD in computer-assisted quilting and embroidery formats)

Write here.

Layout idea

JSBK9000 Poppy Feathers Element
(Available on the CD in computer-assisted quilting and embroidery formats)

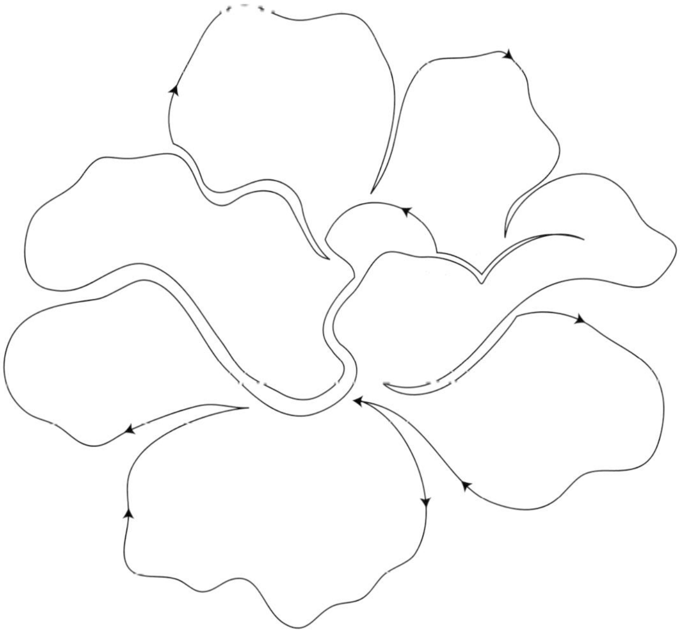

JSBK9000V1 Poppy Feathers Element

JSBK9001 Poppy Feathers Block
(Available on the CD in computer-assisted quilting and embroidery formats)

JSBK9001V4 Poppy Feathers Block

JSBK9001V1 Poppy Feathers Block

JSBK9001V2 Poppy Feathers Block

JSBK9001V5 Poppy Feathers Block

JSBK9001V3 Poppy Feathers Block

Write here.

Layout idea

JSBK9001V6 Poppy Feathers Block

JSBK9002V1 Poppy Feathers Block

JSBK9002V4 Poppy Feathers Block

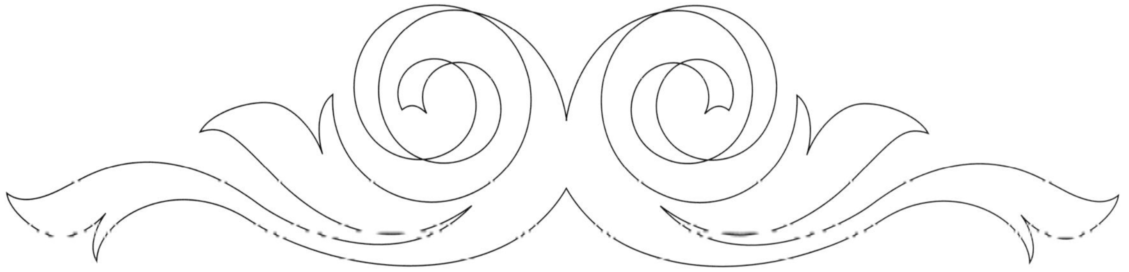

JSBK9002 Poppy Feathers Element
(Available on the CD in computer-assisted quilting and embroidery formats)

JSBK9002V2 Poppy Feathers Block

JSBK9002V5 Poppy Feathers Block

JSBK9002V3 Poppy Feathers Block

Layout idea

Layout idea

JSBK9002V6 Poppy Feathers Block

JSBK9002V7 Poppy Feathers Continuous Triangle
(Available on the CD in computer-assisted quilting and embroidery formats)

JSBKPANTO902 Poppy Feathers Panto

Layout idea

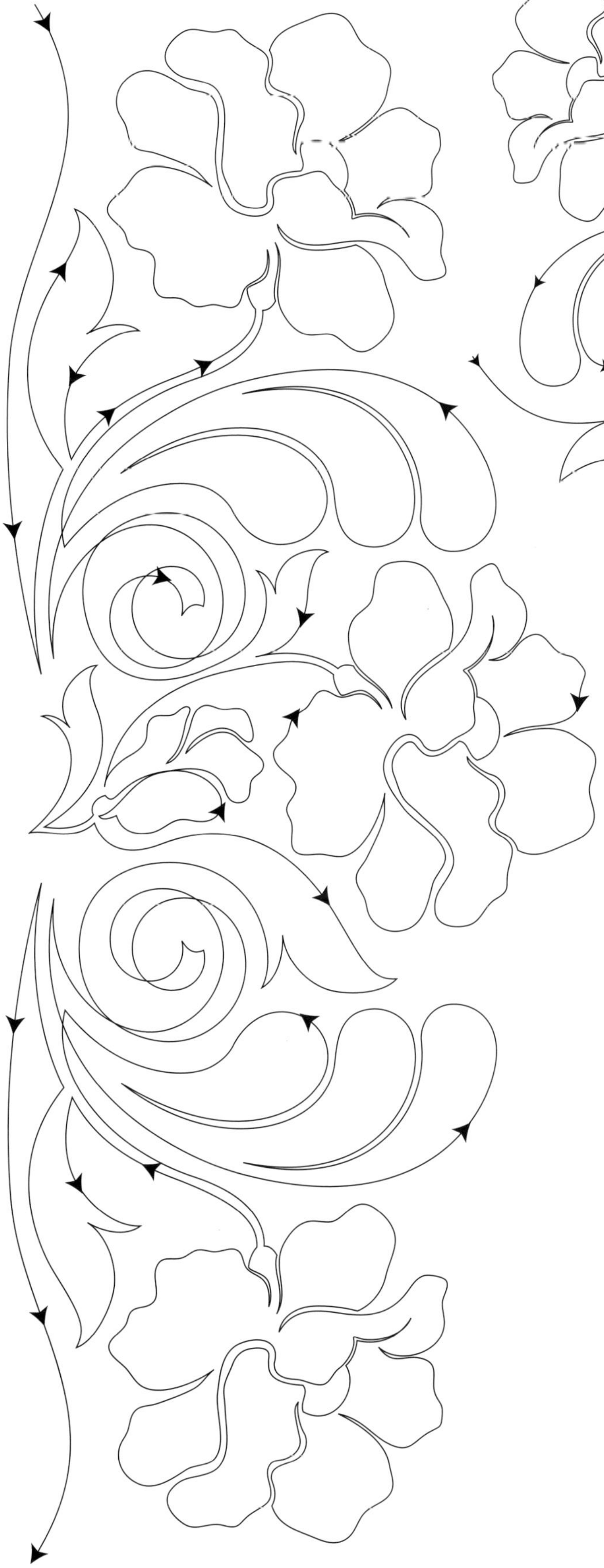

JSBKPANTO901 Poppy Feathers Border

SUITE 10: *Ornamental Leaves Scroll*

Layout idea

JSBK0101 Ornamental Leaves Element
(Available on the CD in computer-assisted quilting and embroidery formats)

JSBK0102 Ornamental Leaves Element 2
(Available on the CD in computer-assisted quilting and embroidery formats)

JSBK0102V1 Ornamental Leaves Block

JSBK0102V2 Ornamental Leaves Kaleidoscope Star

JSBK0102V4 Ornamental Leaves Medallion

JSBK0102V3 Ornamental Leaves Star

JSBK0102V5 Ornamental Leaves Block

JSBK0103V1 Ornamental Leaves Block

JSBK0103V2 Ornamental Leaves Block

JSBK0103 Ornamental Leaves Element 3
(Available on the CD in computer-assisted quilting and embroidery formats)

JSBK0103V3 Ornamental Leaves Block

JSBK0103V4 Ornamental Leaves Block

Layout idea

JSBKPANTO101 Ornamental Leaves Corner & Border
(Available on the CD in computer-assisted quilting and embroidery formats)

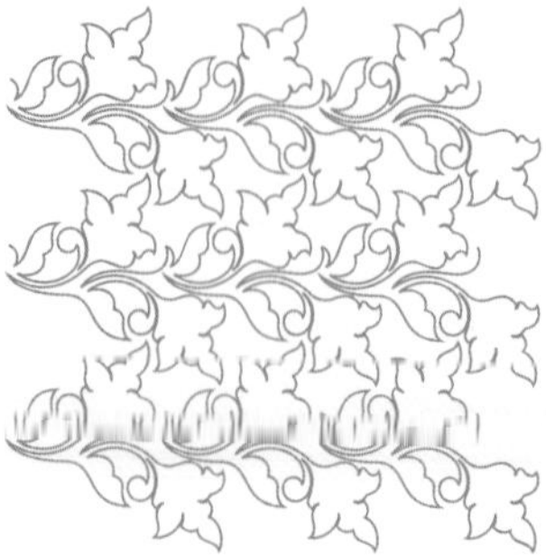

Layout idea

JSBKPANTO102 Ornamental Leaves Panto

Layout idea

JSBK0103V5 Ornamental Leaves Triangle

JSBK0103V6 Ornamental Leaves Triangle 2

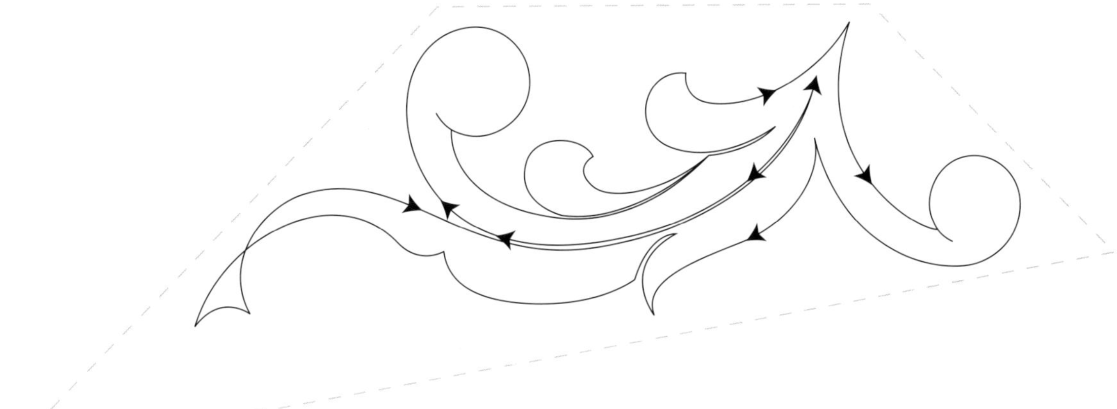

JSBK0103V7 Ornamental Leaves Trapezoid

Appendix

Making Design Patterns and Variations

If the idea of using a computer graphic design program to create your own designs is intriguing to you, then you might like hearing about how I create designs. The process is sort of organic to me. I start out with some basics, and they grow. I usually start with a theme or a doodle that fits into a shape that I know I can repeat to make more designs. The shape you start with is important because it serves as a framework. If you can mirror, rotate, and manipulate a shape to create new blocks, then whatever you draw inside of the shape can be manipulated in the same way. You can think of this as being similar to designing a pieced block. The shapes you use to create a pieced block will be filled with quilting designs, so it makes sense to start with those types of shapes. A wedge from a hexagon, a circle, a square, or a triangle—all of these are good starting shapes.

Progression of Line to Design

I usually begin with a triangle or a wedge and draw inside the shape. If I just want to mirror once, then the lines can start and end on the same side of that shape. Here I started with a curved line that starts and stops on the same vertical axis.

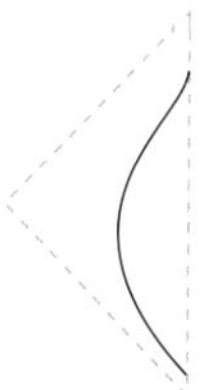

Start and end on same vertical axis.

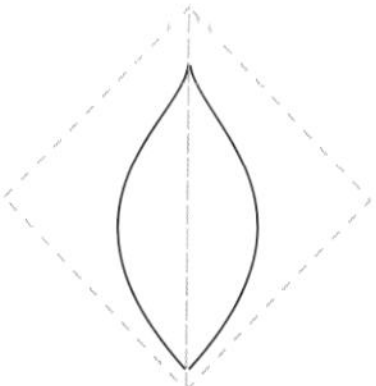

Line with vertical reflection

If I want to mirror and/or rotate, I start the line on one side and end it on the other side of the shape. Here I pulled the bottom of the line out to the side of the triangle.

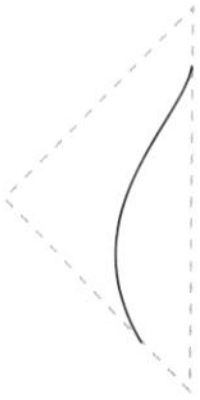

Start and end on different edges.

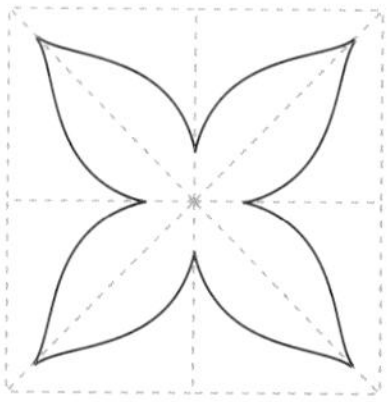

Copy, reflect, then multiply four times around center.

In this example I took the original line (blue), copied it, reflected it, pasted it to the base of the first line, and then reduced it by 50% (red). I then rotated it.

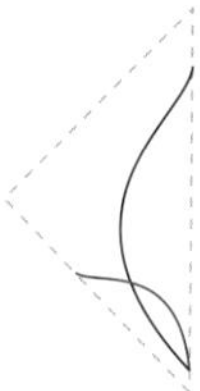

Copy one element and change scale to add new line.

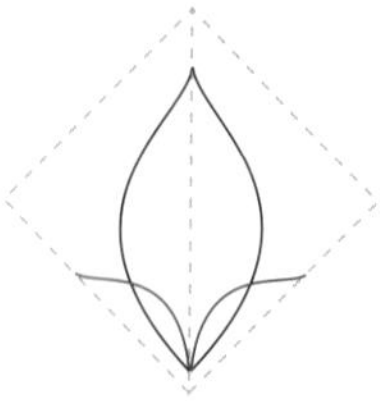

Original line and vertical reflection

After joining, this reflected shape can form a repeating design, or pantograph. With a 90° rotation, the shape can turn a corner for a border. I've offset the second row of this simple repeating pattern to avoid big gaps when doing the next row. The offset is 50%, so one row needs an even number of repeats and the alternate row needs an odd number of repeats. Then the rows are aligned to each other on the vertical center.

You can also copy this simple shape four times and rotate the copies around the center to create a pattern in a square.

Then make a copy of the basic design of the pattern in a square, and rotate the copy 45° to place on top of the original, creating a more complex pattern.

So from a simple line and some basic modifications, you can create four patterns. You can continue with this type of manipulation, changing the angle or tails a little, changing the number of repeats to six, or increasing them to sixteen. More repeats would increase the design complexity to present a lacy-looking pattern.

Progression of a Simple Motif

Here is an example of creating simple motifs from a basic line shape.

1. Create a simple line pattern.

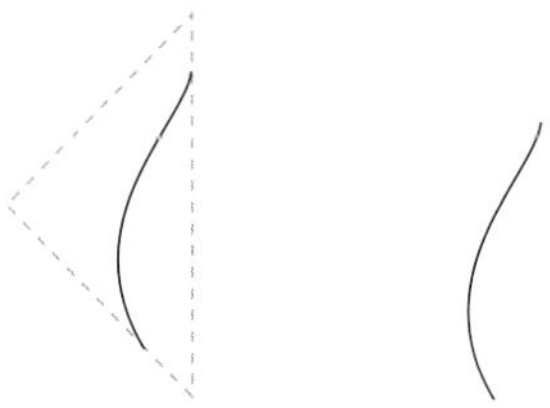

2. Copy and reflect it vertically.

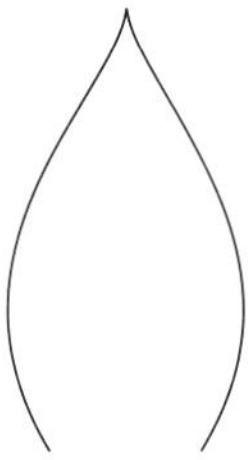

3. Make 4 copies of it and rotate each 90° around the center.

4. Make a copy of the complete shape and rotate the copy 45° on top of the original.

5. There are many easy ways to manipulate the shape. Start with the shape from Step 2.

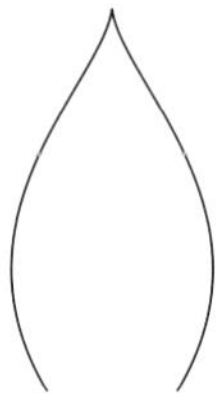

6. Copy it and rotate the copies 30° around the center. Note that this pattern also plays with the overlap in different ways.

7. Or use 6 copies and rotate the copies 60° around the center.

8. You can use 2 copies of the previous shape, rotating one 30°, and then align them vertically and horizontally on top of each other.

Progression of Pantographs (Repeating Patterns)

Designing a repeating pattern, such as a pantograph or border, is similar to designing a motif, but it has a few additional steps.

AN IMPORTANT DETAIL

The most important part of a repeating pattern such as this is that the start and end points of the repeat have to be on the same horizontal plane.

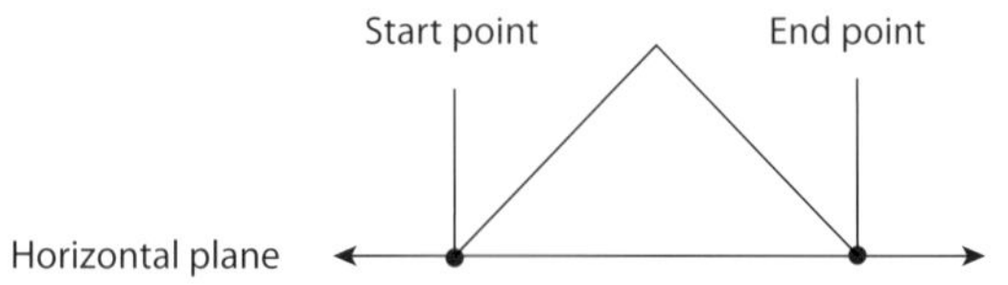

This design will repeat correctly.

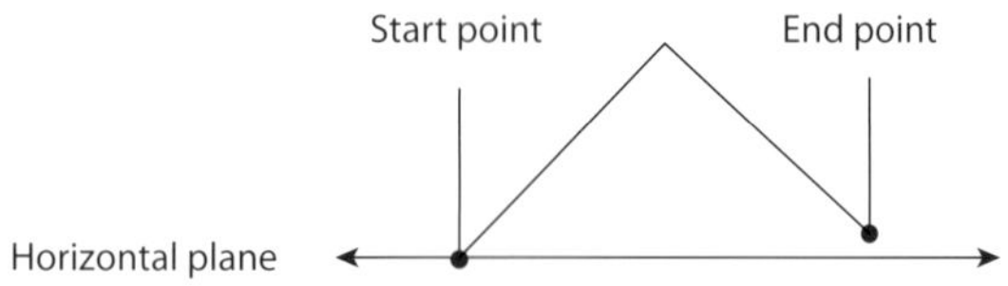

This design will *not* repeat correctly.

This is a case where perfect matters. When a designer gets the end points close but not perfectly aligned to each other on the same horizontal plane, the pattern can drift up or down.

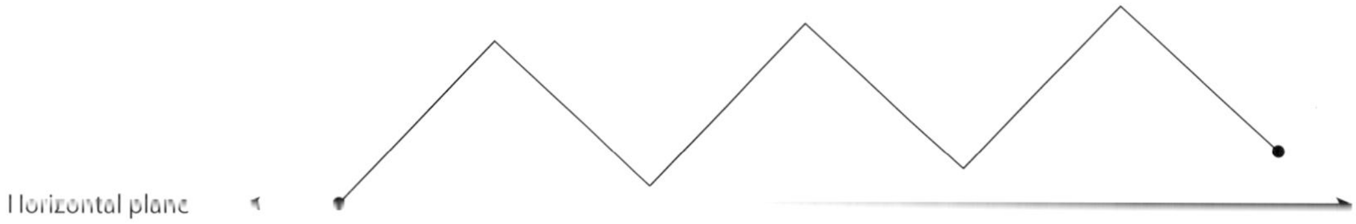

This is important—a little difference can make a big difference because of the multiplication of the error. Here's the math: If an end point is 0.05″ off and a pattern repeat is 10″ long with the width to be quilted 100″, the pattern will be ½″ off by the time it reaches the far end of the quilt. That's a noticeable difference.

WALKING THROUGH THE REPEAT DESIGN

1. Start with the original shape.

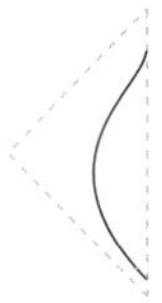

2. Copy and reflect the original.

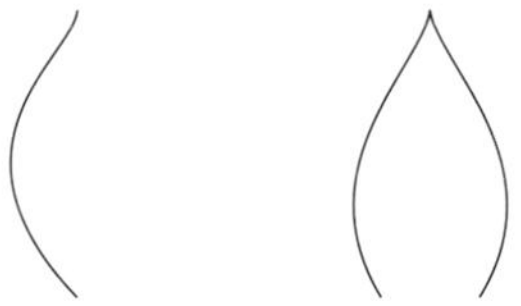

3. Make 2 copies of the shape, reducing the size of one of them 50%.

4. Touch the start of the small copy to the end point of the larger version, overlapping the 2 shapes.

5. Repeat the design several times.

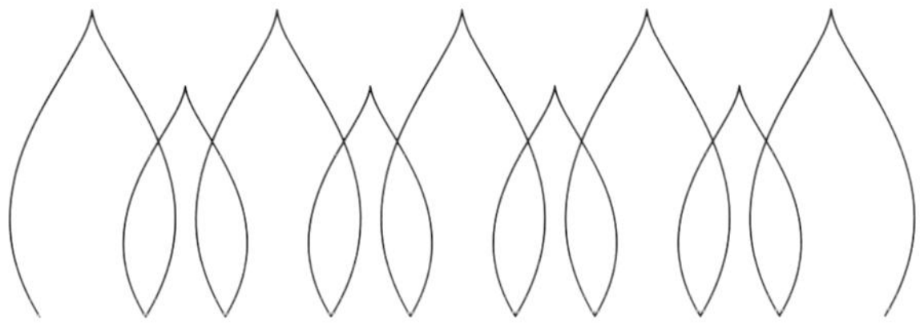

ADDING VARIATION

To make more variations, you might want to add more lines. The red line is what I added, checking to make sure that my transition from the original element to the new line is smooth.

Then I reflected the element to create a leafy look (followed through in the green). With the one leaf up and one down, an offset spacing will allow the pattern to interlock, so that the quilting density is similar overall.

In this case, I still think it could be better and there is room for me to add a smaller leaf between each pair of the bigger leaves.

CREATING TESSELLATIONS

A tessellation is created when a shape is repeated over and over again, covering an area without gaps or overlaps. Any tessellating shape will work for a template to draw a pantograph pattern that interlocks. Some tessellations are more successful than others. You don't need to fill the tessellating shape completely with a drawing. It's okay to leave some breathing room for the design. The shape just serves as a guide for your drawing so that you don't make a pantograph that has either large holes with no quilting or areas with overlapping or bumping rows.

Regular shape that can tessellate

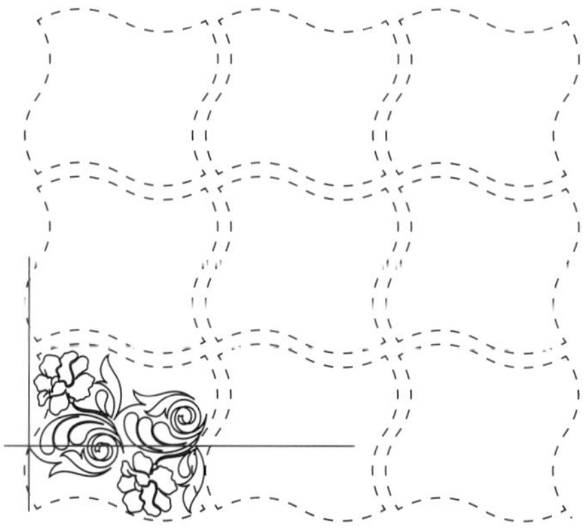

Tessellation with design pattern

You can also create tessellations with irregular shapes. These will still work as a framework to create a design for a pantograph. For successful pantographs, the horizontal and vertical corners of the tessellating shapes should be on the same plane. If they are not on the same plane, the pattern repeats will have to be offset from one row to another, which can be more challenging for quilters to line up.

In the examples below, the red lines show how the corners of each tessellating shape either line up or don't line up along the same plane. In this example the tessellating shape looks uniform, but the starts are not on the same vertical plane and each row is offset.

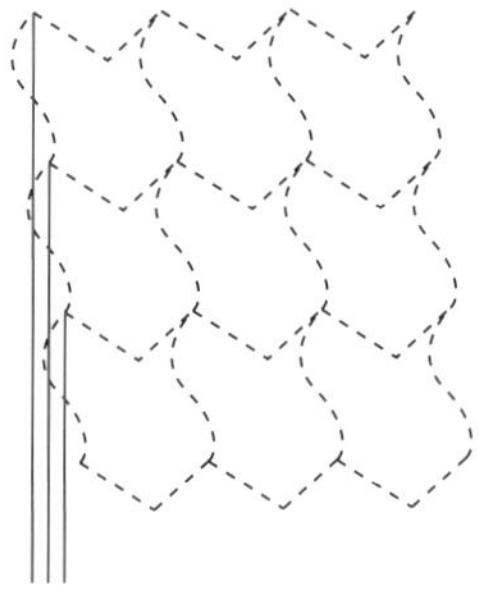

Starting points are *not* on same vertical plane.

Although the next example looks more irregular, it is better than the previous example because all the corners line up on the same horizontal and vertical planes. Creating patterns within these types of templates allows for rows that do not have to be offset, and this is the easiest type of pantograph pattern for quilters to lay out.

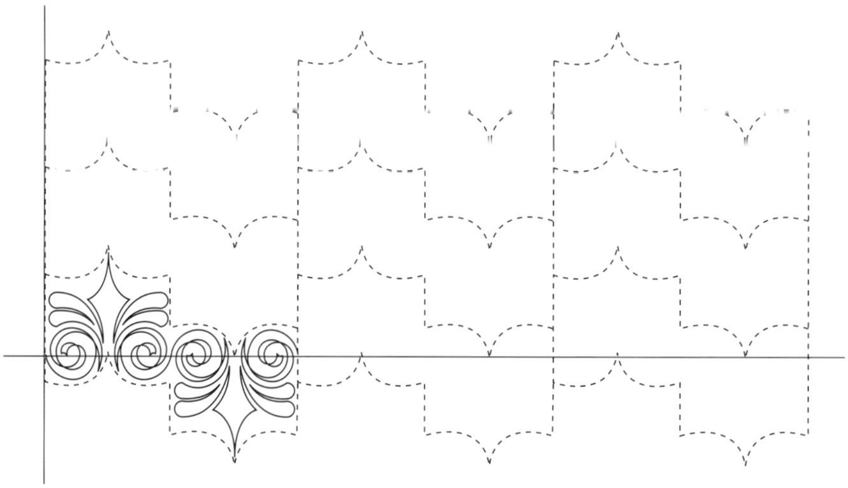

Tessellation pattern starting and stopping on same planes

PANTOGRAPHS THAT WORK

Keep in mind that successful pantographs will have the following characteristics:

- The shapes will interlock.
- The quilting will have relatively even spacing—no super-dense areas combined with very open spaces.
- Patterns are paper-friendly and need less backtracking, which uses less thread and less time. Paper-friendly patterns (meaning friendly to quilters who use paper patterns and not computerized pattern files) have little or no backtracking so they can be easily followed with a laser light or stylus. A pantograph generally is meant to be a pattern that can be sewn more quickly than a complex pattern. It's also faster than custom quilting. People often use pantographs because they need or want to get the quilting done in a timely manner. Therefore, patterns that are paper-friendly are also friendlier to those quilters who are using pantograph patterns.
- And most importantly, the start and end must be on the same horizontal plane.

Resources

Common quilting and sewing supplies are available from local sewing, quilting, and craft stores as well as online.

Adobe adobe.com
Graphic design software: Illustrator, Photoshop, Photoshop Elements

Apache OpenOffice openoffice.org
Computer graphic design program Draw (free to download)

American Professional Quilting Systems apqs.com
Information and locations of local dealers
APQS Millennium, APQS Lucey,
7Quilt Path computerized quilting system

Art & Stitch artnstitch.com
Computer design software for quilting and embroidery design

Auntbeasquilts search on eBay.com
This eBay seller is a source for purchasing quilt tops.

Baby Lock babylock.com
Information and locations of local dealers
Enterprise 10-needle embroidery machine, Baby Lock 3 oz. Super Stable Stabilizer, No-Show Mesh Fusible Stabilizer, Tear-Away Stabilizer, Dissolve-Away Mesh Backing

Chippewa Sewing Machine Co. (Mike Figmiller) chippewasewing.com
My local Baby Lock and Singer dealer, who has always taken care to provide me with the best service and embroidery and sewing machines

CorelDRAW coreldraw.com
Computer graphic design software

Derwent Inc. pencils.co.uk
Available at art and craft supply stores worldwide
Inktense watercolor pencils

Fil-Tec Threads bobbincentral.com
Glide, Perish, Essence, Allure, and Premo-Soft threads; Magna-Glide prewound bobbins; Eco Wash stabilizer; variety of backings and topping for embroidery

General Pencil Company generalpencil.com
Available at art and craft supply stores
Sketch & Wash pencil, White charcoal pencil, Color-Tex pencils

Inkscape inkscape.org
Computer graphic design software (free to download)

IntelliQuilter / KasaWorks, LLC intelliquilter.com
IntelliQuilter computerized quilting system

Kiss-Off Inc. kissoff.com
Also available from generalpencil.com
Kiss-Off Stain Remover stick

Marshall Dry Goods marshalldrygoods.com
Tall Cotton Quilting Solids and general-purpose fabrics

Pilot Pen pilotpen.us
Also available at office supply stores
FriXion pen

Quilters Dream Batting quiltersdreambatting.com
Available at many sewing, quilting, and craft supply stores
Quilters Dream Wool, Quilters Dream Puff, Quilters Dream Cotton, Midnight Dreams Black Poly

Sakura Color Products of America Inc. sakuraofamerica.com
Available at many art and craft supply stores
Gelly Roll white gel ink pen and Pigma Micron pens

Superior Threads superiorthreads.com
Also available at many sewing, quilting, and craft supply stores
So Fine! thread

About the Author

Jessica Schick is an artist who thought her career would be teaching art. Then she bought a longarm quilting machine. Within a month she was considering quilting for hire and teaching quilting rather than pursuing a career in public education. She was designing her own quilting patterns, so she would still be using her drawing and creative skills. And it would allow her to continue to stay home with her children. With the support of her husband, she dove in and began quilting for customers full time, averaging 300 to 350 quilts each year. After researching the limited opportunities available to designers in the computer-assisted quilting market, she started Digi-Tech Designs (digitechpatterns.com). Her goal is to provide excellent-quality designs with the customer's and designer's needs being the primary concern. She now designs patterns for quilting, embroidery, and other crafts. And she wrote a book! She lives in Wisconsin with her husband.

Great Titles and Products

from C&T PUBLISHING

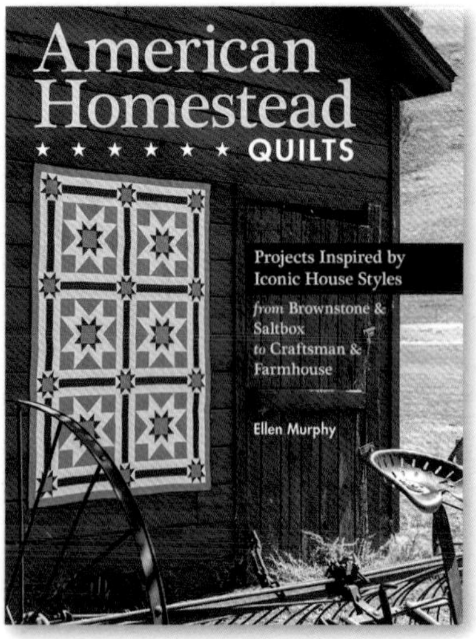

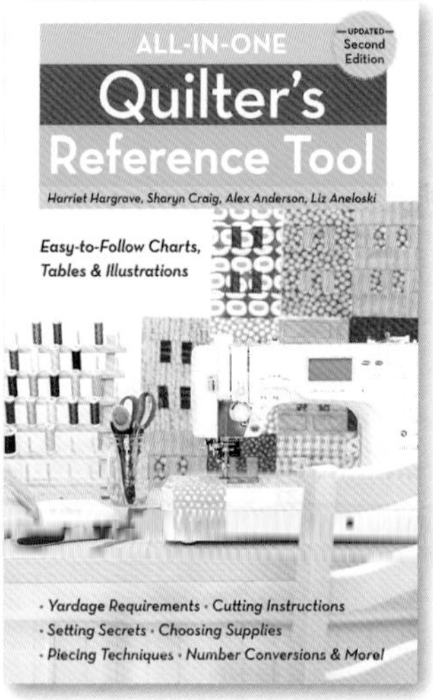

Available at your local retailer or **ctpub.com** *or* **800-284-1114**

For a list of other fine books from C&T Publishing, visit our website to view our catalog online.

C&T PUBLISHING, INC.
P.O. Box 1456
Lafayette, CA 94549
800-284-1114
Email: ctinfo@ctpub.com
Website: ctpub.com

Tips and Techniques can be found at ctpub.com/quilting-sewing-tips.

For quilting supplies:

COTTON PATCH
1025 Brown Ave.
Lafayette, CA 94549
Store: 925-284-1177
Mail order: 925-283-7883
Email: CottonPa@aol.com
Website: quiltusa.com

Note: Fabrics shown may not be currently available, as fabric manufacturers keep most fabrics in print for only a short time.